LETTERS FROM THE
PEACE CORPS

LETTERS FROM THE
PEACE CORPS

Selected and edited by

IRIS LUCE

ROBERT B. LUCE, INC.

Washington, D.C.

LETTERS FROM THE PEACE CORPS

COPYRIGHT © 1964 BY ROBERT B. LUCE, INC.

All rights reserved, including the right to reproduce
this book, or parts thereof, in any form, except for
the inclusion of brief quotations in a review.

Second Printing, August 1964

LIBRARY OF CONGRESS CATALOG CARD NUMBER: 64-18388

MANUFACTURED IN THE UNITED STATES OF AMERICA

VAN REES PRESS • NEW YORK

Schultz - Holmes Memorial Library
Blissfield, Michigan

To the memory of

PRESIDENT JOHN F. KENNEDY

who, by establishing the Peace Corps,

inspired a new generation of Americans

to unselfish public service.

Acknowledgments

The editor and the publisher wish to express thanks to the following Peace Corps volunteers, who gave permission for their words to be quoted in this book:

Joe T. Adair
Barnett Chessin
Kenneth M. Clark
John Coyne
George DeWan
Ella Doran
Nancy Susan Dunetz
Bosanka Evosevic
Jacob Feldman
James F. Fisher
Rosemary George
Jim Gregory
Susan M. Johnson
William Kornblum

Roger Landrum
Walter M. Langford
A. W. Lewis, Jr.
Fred McCluskey
Melinda Meyer
Carolyn M. Minto
Preston K. Minto
Thomas Peyton
Elizabeth Roseberry
Thomas J. Scanlon
Angelica Simmons
William F. Woudenberg
Arnold Zeitlin
Marian Zeitlin

Contents

INTRODUCTION

It was my good fortune one evening to be seated with the wife of Senator J. William Fulbright, whose daughter was working here in Washington at Peace Corps Headquarters. Mrs. Fulbright suggested that someone should compile a collection of letters from Peace Corps volunteers in the field to give Americans a firsthand report on the triumphs and the hardships that these people have experienced while working in the Corps. So to her goes the credit of being the "mother" of this book.

After some negotiation, Peace Corps officials in Washington approved the idea and we began the task of reading the thousands of letters that Peace Corps men and women have written home explaining their work, their living conditions, their frustrations, and their accomplishments in the Corps.

Some of these letters were written directly to friends at home, others to the Peace Corps Headquarters itself; some were written to fellow volunteers, others to parents.

The letters are an inspiring and remarkable collection.

Please do not turn down the corners of the pages. Use a book mark.

They have the freshness of discovery and the immediacy that comes from daily personal contact with the living conditions, the economic conditions, and the people of other societies far different from our own. In them, we believe, you will see a spirit of pioneering accomplishment on the part of these volunteers that should be a source of great pride to all Americans.

A note on the manner in which the letters appear: They are all used with the permission of their authors, but to avoid any possible complications in "host" countries, the letters are published anonymously. We have added a minimum of editorial comment, preferring to let the volunteers tell their stories in their own words.

We owe a debt of gratitude to the Peace Corps officials who made it possible for us to assemble this volume and, of course, to those volunteers who unknowingly wrote this book.

IRIS LUCE

Washington, D. C.
February, 1964

LETTERS FROM THE
PEACE CORPS

CHAPTER I

"I Want to Work for Something Important..."

Shortly after presidential candidate John F. Kennedy promised, in a speech in San Francisco, that if elected he would establish a "peace corps", a trickle of letters began flowing into the Kennedy headquarters from those who wanted to be first on the volunteer list.

That trickle became a torrent after Kennedy was elected. Before the Peace Corps offices were officially open, a stack of more than twenty thousand letters was waiting to be opened.

These letters of inquiry have never stopped coming. As this is written, the second wave of Peace Corps volunteers is being selected and the number of volunteers serving overseas is being raised to ten thousand. Curiosity about this first governmental "peace army" seems to have no limit. Today, the letters come to the Peace Corps Headquarters at the rate of approximately five thousand every week. They come from every part of the United States; from young and old; from teachers, doctors, nurses, architects, lawyers, auto mechanics, and, yes:

> "Kindly furnish information as to occupations needed by the Peace Corps. Would jazz musicians be of any interest?"

The truth of the matter is that any applicant over eighteen who has no dependent children under eighteen is eligible to apply for the Peace Corps. Married or single, college-educated or not, any American who meets these requirements and volunteers for work abroad is carefully considered by the Peace Corps selection board.

When the letters were opened, Corps officials realized that they had touched a responsive nerve in the American heart:

> "I want to work for something I feel is important to mankind and not just 'putting in my eight hours' as I am now doing."

There were letters from men who wanted to get away from their wives (and wives who wanted to get away from their husbands), letters from young children:

> "I read about the people the Peace Corps has in the different countries around the world. . . . I really envy them and their work. I am sixteen and a junior in high school . . .

and from retired and older people who saw in the Peace Corps a chance to be useful workers once again:

". . . my wife and I are told so often that we are too old for jobs in the present economy that we are both kind of disgusted. But haven't given up hope of finding something. We have discussed the Peace Corps a number of times, and have finally decided to inquire directly. . . ."

The majority of letters, however, came from the young people of the nation—between twenty and twenty-five years old. Eighty percent of the inquiries were from people under thirty. About three out of every five letters came from men, and 90 percent of all the letters came from single men and women. Four out of five had had some college training, and about half had graduated from college.

At a moment when the American youth was being generally cuffed around in the press and elsewhere as soft, materialistic or delinquent, the response to the idea of the Peace Corps demonstrated that someone had overlooked the fact that if given the chance—if given a direction— there was a boundless supply of energy, idealism, and enthusiasm:

"I hope to do my best to be of any possible help to another human being who can use it."

"I hope to assist as best I can to help other peoples to help themselves."

"We must work side by side with the people of these countries, eating their food, living in humble quarters as the people live in, and working with their equip-

3

ment. We must realize that being an American is no basis for special privileges."

"I would like very much to join the Peace Corps. . . . I would particularly like to know in what countries teachers are needed and what the requirements are."

"We have so much and others have so little. May I help someone less fortunate than myself, giving them my time, my effort, my knowledge and my enthusiasm?"

As the letters arrived in a steady stream, the evidence was clear—that the Peace Corps had caught the imagination of a good many Americans, young and old, and that it would satisfy a number of unfilled yearnings.

By actual analysis, the most frequent reason given in the letters of inquiry for wanting to join the Corps was "to help other people." The idea that at long last one could take a personal hand in alleviating the poverty and backwardness of other areas of the world, that there was an alternative to the doling out of "foreign aid" on the one hand and putting on an Army uniform on the other, had tremendous appeal:

"I wish to make the Peace Corps part of my conscientious effort in behalf of the peace race. . . ."

"The Peace Corps seems an ideal way for me to serve my country and to be of assistance to other people . . . it is not a charity or relief organization that hands out money, but lends its people. . . ."

4

Many applicants saw it as their personal opportunity to correct the false image of America abroad:

"I hope to be a vocal member of the community I join and try to dispel the notion that the United States is a nationalistic power intent only on protecting its own interests."

Again:

"Having seen and heard of many Americans (diplomats and tourists) who have created bad impressions of the United States abroad, I am challenged to prove to the rest of the world that all Americans are not rich or imperialistic or snobs."

Not all applicants were motivated by such idealism. Some saw in the Corps a chance to learn a foreign language, others an opportunity to travel, others a new educational experience, and some a chance to get away from the routine of their lives. Perhaps the most remarkable letter of this kind follows:

"This letter is an appeal for you to help J—— and me as well as helping our country. All our lives we have been pampered. Our fathers paid our way through college, and when we finished we ran back to them to live. We have developed a feeling of being parasites in this society.
Thus we are writing to ask you to arrange an appointment for us in the Peace Corps in some foreign land, such as Nigeria. You will not have to be afraid of our running home to our father and mother if you take

our return tickets and give us only enough money to buy essentials.

If we do not accept the first offer, because we do not have the courage to leave our fathers and mothers, please keep offering contracts to us until we do accept."

For a good many applicants, the Peace Corps seemed to be an ideal training ground for future work or studies and a practical way to test one's knowledge, skill, or stamina:

"I hoped to gain first hand knowledge of people, language, and customs of Latin America as a basis for additional studies."

"The Peace Corps gives me a chance to 'look around' before deciding on a career."

"Serving with this group would also give me a chance to test some of my beliefs...that I am understanding, can live with less, not a cultural stereotype, and can face unique and challenging situations."

One applicant made his reasons perfectly plain:

"I would like to study the Corps for material for a novel I would like to write."

Through letter after letter, the evidence became clearer that the Peace Corps had become a goal for thousands and thousands of Americans. One is impressed by the variety in those who applied, the skills that were offered, and the earnest desire to be of service to humanity in what seemed to be a tangible way. Here, for the first time, was an opportunity to cut through that frustrating, indirect relationship of nation to nation and work on a people-to-people basis.

Finally, the applicants expressed some of the American conscience, the guilt we feel as one of the "have" nations in a world of "have nots". This letter verged on the poetic:

"... I also hope to find some sort of personal peace, to salve my conscience that I and my peers were born between clean sheets when others were issued into the dust with a birthright of hunger. Perhaps afterward when I hear the cry of humanity I shall be unashamed that I am not of that cry, because I helped to still a part of it."

CHAPTER II

Training for
the Job Ahead

*W*ith the problem of preparing the newly recruited volunteers for overseas duty, the Peace Corps found itself faced with its second imponderable. Rarely, in our national experience, had Americans been trained on such short notice to perform such a random variety of jobs in so many different and remote areas of the world.

To be sure, some private agencies, such as the Experiment in International Living and various other groups, had been involved in providing orientation for overseas work but, for the Peace Corps itself and its pioneering plans, no one precedent could serve as a guide for volunteer training.

For its training program, the Peace Corps turned primarily to the universities for help. Of the first 1,150 volunteers, almost all were sent in the summer of 1961 to a university training center.

This group of Americans would be scrutinized abroad and at home by doubters and cynics. How could they be taught on a crash basis enough practical skills, information, and orientation to prepare them for what was essentially a task of unknown dimensions?

Surely language training must be a part of the curriculum and endless amounts of history, sociology, orientation in the look, the ideas, the customs, and habits of strange people. Physical training, first aid, hygiene—none of these could be taken for granted.

And of course, this was the first time that the volunteers had an opportunity to meet their fellow workers—the others who were engaged in the experiment.

Their reactions to the training program, by and large, were good. Most made proper allowance for the fact that this was a new and rushed program, that taken as a whole, the training program did what it was supposed to do—prepare them to operate effectively abroad.

This girl later found herself teaching French in Ghana:

"Training began for Ghana II at the University of California in June. We were extremely fortunate to have an outstanding faculty of knowledgeable, experienced, perceptive, inspiring experts on Ghana and Africa to guide our learning. I would venture the opinion that the intensity and caliber of the instruction can be directly correlated with the effectiveness and overall performance of the Peace Corps volunteer in his assignment overseas. (Of course the individual himself also plays a very important part!) The fact that there are so few 'washouts' in the field is indicative of the responsible, worthwhile, relevant train-

9

ing Peace Corps volunteers are being given before embarking on their assignments. Our eight-week program ran on a five-and-one-half-day class week beginning at 8:00 A.M. and usually ending around 10:00 P.M., with time out for lunch and dinner. In addition to this rigorous class schedule, we managed to read extensively and compile several projects.

"The major emphasis of our studies was Ghana, education in Ghana (since we will all be teachers), and Africa in general. Although instruction in schools is in English, the official language of the country (Ghana was under British rule as the Gold Coast until independence in 1957), we received daily instruction in Twi from Twi-speaking Ghanaians. Twi is the dominant vernacular of approximately fifty languages and dialects spoken in Ghana.

"Attention was also given to courses titled American Studies and International Studies (an attempt to make us better-informed Americans and world citizens), benefiting from the participation of Cal professors in these lecture-discussion sessions.

"Another aspect of our training was to prepare us for maintaining our personal health and hygiene in an area unblessed with the amenities we take for granted in America. Each of us has a medical kit and is prepared to render emergency treatment. I'm hoping the occasion will not arise when I might be called upon to assist in the delivery of a baby, but for that too we are prepared. A daily hour and a half of physical fitness was designed both to maintain and encourage good physical condition and to familiarize us with the games played by Ghanaian youth, since most of us will also be involved with the athletic program of our schools. (I can't yet claim to be a pro at coaching track and field, but look out for me when I run with that javelin!)

"You might be wondering just what kind of people become engaged in an endeavor of this nature. My impression is that the volunteers are both realistic and idealistic: realistic in the sense that they are aware of the inherent danger in the world situation today and have a deep conviction that Americans must *live* the ideals which they have preached for so long—peace, freedom, equality, individual worth, and human brotherhood; idealistic in their belief and hope that through contributing two years of their life they can assist in some small way in the ultimate realization of these ideals for all mankind. *Cui multum detum* is the inscription we read on our table settings at every meal here at the University of Ghana where we are quartered during this two-week orientation period. Although their reminder is meant for the university students, who form an educated elite in a country which is still over 50 percent illiterate, I feel it is even more appropriate for us. How many warnings we Americans have had in recent years that much *is* required of those to whom so much has been given.

"The average age of the volunteers tends to be around twenty-five, which is understandable since this kind of project is more easily undertaken before one has accepted certain responsibilities. Our group is no exception, except for an experienced male chemistry teacher, age fifty-seven. Although some in our group have advanced degrees and teaching experience, the majority received their A.B. or

B.S. this June. Some of those designated as teachers in technical institutes have no college degree but are qualified for their respective positions on the basis of their practical knowledge and skills. Of the initial eighty-five candidates the ratio of men to women was about 3 to 1 (average for all groups), which seems only natural to a Stanford woman! California, with thirteen trainees, rated highest numerically of thirty-three states represented. Stanford led the universities with seven graduates (four M.A.'s). Other institutions represented include Harvard, Yale, Princeton, MIT, Vassar, Bryn Mawr, Smith, and a diverse assortment of other private and state colleges and universities. Other statistics which may be of interest: five Negroes and one married couple. Most secondary teachers will teach math, science, French, English. Since history and the social sciences were my field of study, I am hoping to be able to teach some subjects in these areas also, in addition to the French courses I have been assigned."

In addition to the training here at home, a number of volunteers go through the training center in Puerto Rico, which is a finishing-off process—with heavy emphasis on rugged living, athletics, and morale building for the immediate take-off to the overseas assignment. It is apparently one of the most successful parts of the Peace Corps training program. Here is a detailed description from a girl who survived the rugged training:

"Puerto Rico was one of the most valuable four weeks of my life and we were real pleased to hear that the training there has become an official part of all Peace Corps training. What is the training?—well, it is more than just a physical training center and we learned more than just to be able to climb mountains or take hikes through the woods. We learned how to look at ourselves and others without the luxuries we're accustomed to and how they react under strain and pressure. I won't say it was an easy four weeks, but then the most valuable things are not the most easily obtained. After living in D.C. and conforming to society in dress, etc., Puerto Rico was a real switch. Up at six each morning doing exercises and running before breakfast, language two to three hours a day, rock climbing, trekking, swimming, and Lord knows what all, but we went till nine or ten each night with only Sunday a.m.'s free. You'd better believe we were ready to "hit the sack" by the end of each day just as soon as we could. We hardly had time to talk to others outside of our group. The instructors at camp are tops. For rock climbing we had Bill B——, one of the top instructors in the country and a guide at the Grand Tetons. He is a well-built, quiet-mannered, and even-tempered person—he has to be because when you first look at those mountains it "ain't" easy to make up your mind to play human fly and just go scooting up. Before that four weeks were up we went up a mountain and rappelled off it as well as a spillway on a dam. Actually it is quite safe and not bad—you just have to decide to do it and that's all—just a matter of mind over body. The dam was about the simplest rappel except for that initial jump. As you know, the distance from the top of the dam to the spillway is a "far piece," more so when you are going off backwards! We always had a belay around

13

our middle so there was no danger. Some times I thought it was harder walking back up to the top! My last time down on the dam the leather pad slipped and I didn't realize it so I got a slight rope burn—nevertheless, it was a good conversation piece, and in twenty years I don't suppose I'll even know the difference—ha!

"Trekking was an experience, too. First we took an all-morning hike, then an all-day that was topped off with an all-day overnight, and then this was climaxed by a three-day hike for the girls, and a four-day for the fellas. We learned which foods we could use from the woods and how to fix them. *Melangia*, a tuber that tastes like a potato, and boiled bananas are the main diet of the country folk and I can't say I liked them, but after walking four hours with a pack on your back it was 'right good eating.' We had topographical maps for all these treks and after our three-day trek, I am not sure of our map-reading ability. We somehow or other got off the trail, but we got to where we were supposed to be going.

"Now to my favorite—the swimming. We really weren't having swim classes, but were being taught a method called drownproofing. Freddie L——, head swim coach at Georgia Tech, was our instructor and a better one couldn't be found. The method is tremendous and why more colleges haven't realized it and started using it is beyond me. I've been swimming since I was four years old, but if you had told me I would learn a method in that four weeks that would enable me to do a resting stroke, or a travel stroke with which I could swim or rest for hours, even days, and come out not tired, I would have said you were crazy. Well, let me tell you what we did.

14

We used this method to do this resting stroke for ten minutes, the travel stroke for ten, a front and back somersault, pick up a ring from the bottom of the pool and swim one width of the pool under water with our hands tied and then with our feet tied. With hands tied you use your teeth to pick up the ring. This was done mostly so that if you ever were caught in an accident or had a cramp and one member of your body was incapacitated you could stay alive, travel, and even save someone else and still not get exhausted. I will admit I never got to the bottom for that ring with my hands tied because we were in a saltwater pool and, as Freddie says, there are some girls who float better than others, especially in salt water (especially those of us with added padding!). We had some practice in lifesaving and again learned another way, or shall we say, the Georgia Tech method. That got to be a favorite expression—if nothing else works, just do the Georgia Tech travel stroke.

"Well, the climax of our swim instruction was to swim two lengths of the pool underwater by entering doing a somersault flip. Average time under water is fifty seconds. I don't guess I need to say more—have you ever tried holding your breath just lying down for that long?—well, we did and thirty-five seconds was the best for the most part of us. Well, all it took was an hour and a half lecture from Freddie, the Georgia Tech method, and us just plain making up our minds to do it, and we had the highest competition record at the camp (especially the girls) which includes having several who had never swum a bit and others who had never jumped in the water on their own accord before. If anyone ever tells you that the mind

15

can't control the physical body, don't you believe it. Just to see some people scared to death (me included) make up their minds to stay under whether they passed out or not (there is no danger if you do, as we were carefully watched), but refusing to give up, was a tremendous experience. As they say, there probably won't be a time in your life when the situation is more complex than at the beginning. It really shows the people who are going to give up under a trying situation and those who will fight it through.

"We also had a week of extension experience in Puerto Rico and this was wonderful. The Puerto Ricans are truly wonderful and hospitable. Even the poorest we met on our treks offered us the use of the few things they had and gave all they had. I dare say the majority of us hated to leave that beautiful and friendly island, but then we were anxious to get to our destination. Might add here that our number had decreased by nine by this time, dropping four in D.C. and five in Puerto Rico. This too is an amazing part of this program's selection committee. They really know each of us backwards and forwards from the day we were born, I do believe, and are they thorough!—truly professional. Although we all hated to see our friends leave the group, we know it was done in the best interests of all. Now we are in the last phase of the training here in Rio where we are living with Brazilian families. Priscilla and I are staying with one of the language teachers and her family. We had spent several weekends there while out at the university, so we were pleased when they requested to have us stay with them. Although two in the family speak English, we only speak Portuguese and now our lectures are entirely in Portuguese. So far the lectures have been excellent and we're really getting a good course on Brazil, its history, culture, customs, extension 4-H Club work, etc. These past four months have truly been an education and worth more than a year in college."

This volunteer found himself teaching in Ethiopia, where he had a chance to summarize his training program at Georgetown University, in Washington, D.C.:

"When I arrived at Georgetown University on July 7, 1962, to begin an eight-week Peace Corps training program in order to teach in the secondary schools in Ethiopia, there were two questions weighing heavily on my mind. They were (1) 'Do I really want to go through with this?' and (2) 'If I do, will the Peace Corps selection board find me qualified to do so?'

"After arriving in Washington, the 325 people who were selected for training were given two and a half days to become settled. The ages of the trainees ranged from eighteen to sixty-seven, the average age being twenty-six. Some 95 percent were college graduates and all were being trained as secondary school teachers although only about 50 percent had had previous teaching experience. On the fourth day the training program began in earnest. All of our time from 6:00 A.M. until 9:00 P.M. was filled with classes six days a week except Monday when we went until midnight. The average day began with thirty-five minutes of rigorous calisthenics and cross-country running. Then, after a big breakfast, we would have two hours of instruction in Amharic, the national language of Ethiopia. The instructors for this course were chosen from among Ethiopian students who were vacationing from their studies in American colleges and universities. This in turn was followed by two hours of either Ethiopian Studies or World Affairs. The Ethiopian Studies component was concerned with the geography, history, government, psychology, sociology, and religion of that nation. World Affairs was a study of contemporary international politics and history administered by the Department of International Relations of Johns Hopkins University. In this course the hour-long lectures were followed by group discussions of the same duration. Each discussion group of about fifteen was guided and intellectually provoked by a member of the Johns Hopkins faculty. Then we had an hour for lunch.

"At 1 p.m. the daily routine was resumed. For the first four weeks of the program the next two hours were devoted to instruction in the individual's major field: i.e., that which he or she would presumably be called upon to teach in Ethiopia on the basis of his previous experience. In my case this meant English. Since I would be teaching English as a foreign language in much the same way as a teacher of French or Latin in an American secondary school, the emphasis in this course was on modern linguistic theory and its application to the English language. This course was followed by one hour of instruction in teaching methodology which was designed especially for those like myself who had little or no previous teaching experience. The only exception to this was on Tuesdays when instead of studying teaching methodology we gathered with a small group of about twelve to vent problems and complaints in the presence of a professionally sympathetic but unobtrusive psychologist. During the second half of the training program my studies in linguistics were replaced by a course in American Studies, which was a combination of history, literature, government, art, and sociology.

"At four it was time for what came to be known during the training program as 'fun and games.' Like the first class of the day, this too was administered by the physical education department at Georgetown. 'Fun and games' included cross-country running, soccer, volleyball, softball, and gymnastics. All of this would have been enjoyable at another time and place, but after having been on the go continually since 6:00 A.M. most of us would have thought an hour-long nap preferable. After working up a fairly decent appetite on the athletic field we were allowed to go to dinner.

"Three days a week, on Tuesday, Thursday, and Saturday, from 6:00 to 7:00 P.M., I had to meet with a small group for practice teaching. Here we would take turns in applying what had been taught in our linguistic theory and teaching methodology lectures. From seven to nine each night we would hear guest lecturers in either Ethiopian Studies or World Affairs. Every night but Monday this would mean the end of the day's scheduled program, and my roommate and I had our choice of either trying to study Amharic vocabulary or simply damning the whole thing and slipping out for a few quick beers before we automatically fell asleep at 10. As a rule, psychological necessity prompted us to choose the latter. On Monday nights, however, there were no lectures. Instead we were required to attend a two-hour session of first-aid instruction followed by instruction in survival swimming, which with about 325 people lasted until midnight.

"With a few exceptions this was the usual routine at Georgetown. Guest speakers for the various courses included Chester Bowles, Elspeth Rostow, and David Riesman. During the last two weeks of the training program, some of the courses were curtailed in order to accommodate a course outlining the medical hazards we would be liable to encounter in Ethiopia. Thursday evenings were given over to the Georgetown medical staff for vaccinations, which we received at the rate of about two per week. We were also given extensive dental treatment of rather dubious quality by the Georgetown School of Dentistry. As an added feature to the program we were required to go on a weekend twenty-five-mile 'survival' hike along the Appalachian Trail. Like much of the overall program, I believe this was intended to serve primarily as deliberate harassment in order to test the individual's psychological stability.

"During the last week the selection boards met frequently to determine which people would find their relationship with the Peace Corps harmful to either themselves, the Peace Corps, or both. When it came time to disband from Washington for a five-day home leave departing for Ethiopia on September 5, only 270 of the original 325 trainees remained. Some left because they voluntarily became disenchanted with the Peace Corps, and others left because they were asked. I found those who were about to go abroad a very diverse, interesting, and reasonably competent group of Americans. Although a surprisingly large number were from among the best colleges and universities in the nation, there were some whose academic credentials and abilities seemed to me to be something less than astounding. They were white people, black people and yellow people; they were wild-eyed liberals and Goldwater conservatives; they were rich and poor; and they advocated segregation and intermarriage. The only two things they had in common were having undergone a training program in the same university and the expectations of spending the next twenty-two months teaching school in a land that just a few years ago was brought 'kicking and screaming into the 15th century.'"

Still another group was in training for Nepal. An English teacher describes his training for this assignment:

"In the middle of final examinations last Spring I suddenly found myself forced into deciding what would happen to me in the cold cruel world lying outside Princeton, New Jersey: graduate study in anthropology at the University of Chicago, or a two-year hitch with the Peace Corps in Nepal, the tiny Himalayan Kingdom sandwiched between Tibet and India. In the irrational way that I seem to make all the really important decisions, I chose what I later saw advertised as the 'Land of Yeti and Everest.'

"The day following graduation I began training an average of twelve hours per day at George Washington University, in Washington, D.C. About half the time was concentrated on language study, the other half on world

21

Schultz - Holmes Memorial Library
Blissfield, Michigan
WITHDRAWN

affairs, American studies, and Nepal area studies. The quality of the training program, though shoddy in isolated areas, was surprisingly high, particularly in language training. The entire grueling process was made more pleasant than it would otherwise have been by the strong incentive to learn and the usually boundless enthusiasm of my fellow trainees, most of whom were college graduates. After two months we were all graduated, and I was somewhat shocked when I was asked to give a commencement address—in Nepali! This somehow made the Latin Salutatory at Princeton seem rather pedestrian in comparison.

"For life in Nepal, classroom training was not enough, and we soon found ourselves being flown to Denver, where we departed by bus for the Colorado Outward Bound School, located three miles from the ghost town of Marble, Colorado (population of five, according to a recent census). For a month, the day began with an icy dip in a mountain stream at six in the morning, and the rest of the time was filled with hiking, climbing, camping, building bridges, and swinging our way through a 'rope course' consisting of rope ladders, Burma bridge, etc. In one three-day period I walked forty miles and climbed a 13,000 foot peak each day—all with a fully-equipped pack on my back. Somehow I survived.

"Two days later we were in Delhi, but because of the monsoon storms we were stranded there for a week before we could get into Kathmandu, Nepal's capital and the only city in the country with a concrete runway. This, and a newly completed dirt road which is negotiable at least in dry weather, are the only ways to enter the country.

The monsoon had not yet completely subsided, and the flight was the roughest I have ever experienced. Radio communication is so poor that we did not know until half an hour before landing that we would be able to get through the mountains. Finally, we descended from the cloud cover and at once the vale of Kathmandu appeared, ringed by mountains on all sides—an oasis of fertile land and warmth in the middle of the hilly regions of the Himalayas.

"After two weeks of orientation and not enough more language training, we departed for our posts. I went to Bhadgaon, only eight miles from Kathmandu (forty minutes by jeep)."

For a number of volunteers, the most significant part of the training was the "post graduate" indoctrination that occurred after they arrived in the country which had requested their services. One such program was carried on in Pakistan, where the bulk of the indoctrination was engineered by having the newly arrived volunteer live with a Pakistani family for a short period of time. Here is one report on that experience and the training that led up to it:

"In Pakistan, first on the schedule was a three-week 'homestay' with a Pakistani family in Dacca. I'm sure we all learned more that way about Pakistani homelife and personalities than would have been possible otherwise. There were three girls, three boys, and four servants in my host family and practically a steady stream of visitors. One of the servants was the cook's child, servant for

23

her little two-year-old girl. I got to enjoying the kids (most of the time anyway) but got pretty tired of the visitors. Too many 'how do you like Pakistan' questions. A number of the visitors were quite interesting however. One fellow, a bit of a blowhard, rated the 'colonialists' of Asia. The Americans were the least adept. The British were best, with the Dutch and French following in that order.

"From the all-Pakistani faculty here at the Academy, Comilla, we got an additional three weeks' orientation in Pakistan history and current conditions. Two lectures were especially outstanding I thought. One on 'Society in Rapid Transition' looked at the likelihood of the several classes losing respect and communication with one another as rapid industrial development occurs. This is bound to happen, but if it goes too far, serious bitterness and even hatred may result between the educated and the non-educated. When transition is slower, each stratum tends to accept its lot more, and though there may be dejection there isn't likely to be hatred. The other lecture was on 'underdevelopment' as seen by the ex-colonial countries."

Perhaps it is too early to evaluate the kind of training that would best equip volunteers for their jobs. One brief evaluation, however, came from a volunteer in Sierra Leone, Africa:

"Don't expect training to be the final answer, do not become discouraged, and do what you can to make it better and conserve a personally positive attitude. In

24

general, training is better than you think it is while you are undergoing it. Prof. Worner said we would see bare-chested women in Freetown and we did. We had somehow doubted him. We saw people urinating in the street just as described in the famous postcard incident. We were told to learn the money system. We didn't until we had to barter with a street vendor, and it was embarrassing."

CHAPTER III

Home Away from Home

*I*n the past decade, literally hundreds of thousands of Americans have traveled and lived abroad. Yet very few of them have lived under such a variety of circumstances as the Peace Corps volunteers. It is fair to say that, by and large, of all Americans serving overseas, the Peace Corps volunteers live in the most intimate contact with the citizens of the country in which they are serving. In fact, a good many volunteers live with local families.

The letters from the volunteers capture, in their variety, the reactions to living abroad and describe for others who may follow what it is like to live abroad as a member of the Peace Corps.

In Chile, for example, this couple finds life far better than they had expected:

"Compared to some of the places in which Peace Corps members from the other Chilean group live, we live in castles. We were very lucky to be granted apartments out in the *población* (housing development area) where we are to work. The YWCA was worried about our housing because the government housing agency was not very keen on us using apartments constructed for low-income Chilean families. Not only low income, but not less than four children in each family. As it is, we are being charged double rent. The apartment itself is of a thin brick covered with cement. There is a small oblong kitchen, small back porch, living room, bathroom (with such a small tub that Keith can barely sit in it—knees folded and all), one bedroom with a door, two others divided by a closet, and a small balcony. We are on the fifth floor. To visit others of our group, we must go down five flights of stairs and up five flights.

"For furniture and living items we were given a two-burner stove, a small refrigerator, a table with four chairs (unmistakably red), a bed each (they don't use many double beds in Chile; a woman told me that one reason we in the U.S. had so many divorces was that married couples slept in double beds!), three blankets, four sheets, two pillow cases, three towels, three washcloths, service for six, three pots, a frying pan, and a teakettle. Keith has made some benches and put in a cement sink on the back porch. The sink was given to us by Chilean friends. Up until that time I had washed clothes in the tub by stamping on them with my feet. It really isn't a bad idea and I think it would be excellent exercise for pregnant women. I understand that they wash clothes in Pakistan

27

this way. The only warm water we have is an electrical gadget on the shower and it's not always warm. Keith also built a nice kitchen cabinet and put up curtain rods, the latter a difficult job because of the cement walls. He plans to make doors for the closets and our bedroom, a larger eating table, and a few other items. Little by little, the house is improving.

"From our window you can see the entire *población* of San Gregorio. It has 5,000 houses and 45,000 (rough estimate) people. The homes are of plywood or wood brick. There are five rooms and running water. Each house has about 200 square feet of land for gardens, etc. They are built in sets of two with the plumbing of two houses being back to back. All the people now here lived in the *cayampas* (a Spanish word meaning mushrooms) three years ago. People from the country who came to the city for jobs threw up any type of shelter. Having a home of their own is a completely new idea. Thousands of these lean-to's make a *cayampa*. 'They spring up like mushrooms.'

"Part of the *población* was built on a self-help basis; the foundation and plumbing were already in and the family assigned to the site built their own house with the plywood sheets or wooden bricks. However, self construction was too slow for the government so they stopped it and the other half of the *población* was built entirely by the government housing agency and the families just moved in. You can see the difference between the two sections. Those built on self-help are kept better and families have improved and added onto the houses. Some of them look 'right smart' with the house painted, additions in a well-planned manner, walls around the outside, and flower gardens, vegetable gardens, and chickens. On the other hand, there are many houses that need attention.

"When you first arrive in Chile it seems very similar to the U.S. except for language and eating times—things like that. The buildings are the same, the people dress the same, there are cars, bikes, radios, busses, policemen, airplanes, etc. The climate is much like California, and there is a diversified coloring of the people—from blondes with blue eyes, to those with dark hair and dark eyes. This fools you into thinking that Chileans are much like us. It is what is beneath the U.S. or Chilean suit that counts. The Chileans think differently than we do, have different modes of life; consider other things vital to living; are hurt by different social errors; have a difference of social life; etc. etc. etc. When one finally comes face to face with these differences, one experiences what most people experience living in a foreign country—CULTURE SHOCK. This is a mixture of homesickness for old faces, native language, and familiar ways of doing things and handling people, and frustration with the present situation, inability to see the bright side of things, and a general feeling of 'throwing in the towel.'

"Fortunately I have just passed over the hump of culture shock and am on my way uphill again. Things are brighter, my job is more defined, and my Spanish is improving. I'm catching on to the fundamentals of maneuvering with Chileans, and finding that I really do like Chile and my work. I think that one of the biggest factors in feeling at home in another country is language. You simply cannot communicate without it. At present, I cannot discuss anything of much depth because I cannot really speak that well, but slowly and surely it is coming to me. Sometimes now I catch myself thinking in Spanish and realizing that I've just said something to Keith in Spanish when it was supposed to be said in English—or wake up in the morning and realize my first thought is in Spanish."

In Colombia, on the other hand, things are more primitive. This is from a volunteer who is working with the Colombians in developing better community facilities in the rural areas:

"The *municipio* (township) of Zipacón is a primarily rural community of 3,000 surrounding an urban area (*pueblo*) of 700. The plaza in the center of town is surrounded by stores and houses on two sides and school, church, and municipal buildings on the sides—a typical setup in Latin American towns. There is a mayor, a town council, a health center with a nurse and part-time doctor in attendance, a church, dry-goods stores, sports and social club, and an elementary school (boys and girls separate). The town has water but it's full of germs; it has light only after 6:00 P.M. and the plant frequently fails. There is no hot water, no sewage system. Some houses have latrines, a few, wash basins. Everyone cooks with coal or wood on a crude but adequate stove.

"Our own living conditions are limited by these same inadequacies. We rent a fairly large and new house for 14 U.S. dollars a month with light, toilet, running water, coal stove, kitchen and five rooms. We used to eat in a local restaurant—bananas, potatoes, rice, beef, and yucca for two pesos a meal, and very poorly prepared. We now have our own maid. We can instruct her what foods to buy, how to prepare them, and how to keep a more sanitary kitchen. The maid also washes our clothes and cleans the rooms. The Latin Americans see nothing wrong with having maids and servants even in the poor rural areas. Our main worry is health. Nearly everybody gets diarrhea during his first months in the Colombian *campo*. We have had occasional cases of amoebic dysentery among the volunteers (my partner in Zipacón for instance). But I see no reason why this cannot be controlled by sanitary practices.

"Our work brings us into close contact with Colombians. We work and live together with our Colombian counterpart. He is very dedicated to *Acción Comunal*. He has a wife and eight children to support in Bogotá on an income of about 100 dollars a month (800 pesos); we have only ourselves to support with 1050 pesos a month. This economic injustice is a sensitive point in our relations, and the same problem has been encountered in other work teams. It is not uncommon for the two Americans to be supporting several Colombians as we are in Zipacón (maid, two children, and Colombian co-worker).

"Each member of our team of three knows about the activities of the others. We often work side by side on the same project. We work in close contact with the village priest, a young, dynamic, progressive man who is tolerant of religious differences (Protestant-Catholic). We are somewhat more distant from the municipal government in personal relations although there is necessary collaboration on certain projects. We are closest to the people themselves whom we are trying to help; sometimes we work side by side with pick and shovel, we go to the local fiestas and drink and dance with them, we fraternize in the local stores. We also know the higher government officials in Bogotá connected with community development because we depend on them for technical assistance, and they are our bosses at a distance. At least once a week we take a trip into Bogotá (two hours by train, one hour by car) to visit government and private offices.

"The Peace Corps volunteers in Colombia are in a truly unique position because of our contact with the extremes of the social scale. We are invited into the homes of the richest and most influential families in Colombia while we work with the poorest peasants in the country. This can be a real strain at times because there is so much difference in the two ways of life.

"The Colombians are generally very interested in the Peace Corps, but they don't have the social consciousness to the degree that we have it in the States nor does the government look after its citizens as well as it does in the States. They will support the idea of the Peace Corps but in practice will continue to live within their own social restrictions, reluctant to cross social barriers or sacrifice for the good of the social whole. One young engineer told me that the Peace Corps is several generations in advance of Colombia as far as social service goes, even though Colombians know this is what they ought to be doing more of.

"Naïvely, some Colombians expect a great deal from us, especially here in the rural areas. They think we have come to solve all their problems. At the other extreme they accuse us of being instruments of imperialism. Neither of these extremes, however, expresses the attitude toward the Peace Corps. The attitude tends to be favorable, a mixture of admiration, curiosity, interest, incredulity, doubt, skepticism."

The desirability of living with a family from the host country comes up for discussion in a letter from a thoughtful young member of the Peace Corps in the Philippines. From Concepción, Iloilo, came this communication:

"The main thing I wanted to talk about is my living arrangements. Three years ago, on my first trip abroad, I lived for one semester with an Italian family through the Experiment in International Living. As a former Experimenter yourself, I'm sure you fully understand the significance of that experience, not merely in academic terms but in terms of my total growth and everything that has happened to me since that time. Here in the Philippines, and I imagine in other Peace Corps projects too, the volunteers by and large are living in groups of three or four in their own houses. I was assigned in a lovely group and was quite content and happy until I discovered how much more could be had and how much more could be accomplished. I spent the summer teaching in a rather remote town in the southern part of the Philippines where I was the only volunteer and I lived with a Filipino family. Although I was there for only five weeks, my position in the community and my penetration into Philippine life were so much deeper than before.

When I compare the two situations I realize that in the first one we were always treated as outsiders. True, it was a positive thing; we were treated as guests. But that is not our objective here. In my summer situation my treatment was entirely different, to such an extent that I actually had open conflict with my students who found my teachings rather hard to take and made no bones about letting me know. Having felt my summer experience to be so successful, I requested of Manila that I be transferred to a new community where I could live with a family and be rather isolated from volunteers for the duration of my stay here. The request, of course, was granted. I have been in my new community now for only two weeks. In this short time I have been able to get closer with the children than in the nearly two months I spent at my first post. I analyzed the situation with the family I live with, and we agree that it's because I live with them. When volunteers live together, especially in a group of four, they are cut off from the community. I also find that much of my academic work is accomplished at home, in an informal situation. Two of the members of the family I live with teach in the school I am assigned to. We talk about school problems over the dinner table, and after supper when I work on projects such as science experiments or puppet-making, they join in and pick up some new ideas. There is no doubt in my mind that I have the ideal Peace Corps setup. I realize, of course, that not every volunteer can work effectively in or cope with the type of living conditions I have chosen for myself here. But I certainly hope that more emphasis will be placed on this in the future and that more volunteers will be directly encouraged to live in this way.

"The mosquitoes are getting me and I must end abruptly."

And from remote Trengganu in Malaya, a young nurse writes of her delight with the living accommodations, the people, and her work:

"Ruth and I found this place as lovely as we were told it would be. Our hostel is most certainly a luxury, very open and airy and colorful. We are enjoying the assistant nurses very much because we constantly practice our Malay with them and they usually go into gales of laughter when we say anything. But they are extremely helpful and very patient with us. Ruth is very busy in her surgical ward because there is less staff there. In maternity we have several student midwives so there is less to do but lots to learn.

"Our bicycles arrived and we still are a curiosity when we ride into town, especially for the young children. They are all so alert and inquisitive. Our first trip into town was heralded by the fact that Ruth, who was interested in all the shops and was looking at everything, accidentally rode into a non-moving cyclist and went sailing off her bike. No one was hurt, luckily, but everyone enjoyed it and came out of their shops to see the event. Poor Ruth tried to apologize in Malay.

"We've been enjoying the town and especially the market place. We were taught how to buy pineapples, so now we go in and flick them with our fingers, not really knowing what we're listening for. Everyone thinks we know what we're doing so we have gotten lots of bargains. In pineapples, anyway. We are pretty well settled and have been swimming quite frequently. Haven't made it to the cinema yet. The food is delicious and we're getting fat."

In Nigeria, a Peace Corps volunteer is assigned to St. Catherine's School in Owo. The conditions there are "primitive," but pleasant, she reports:

"Outside of the classroom and taken singularly or in small groups the girls are delightful and enchanting. They have more personality and poise than the teenagers I have taught in the U.S. They are helpful, respectful, obedient, inquisitive, casual, and fun-loving. They rush to carry your books or packages, never hesitate to do an errand, and nod or almost genuflect upon passing you.

"They are awed by the fact that I can sew, that I do my own cooking and cleaning. They are even amazed on the playing field when I show how to put the shot or start a run. (By the way, that Phys. Ed. will come in handy here; don't fight it, for you will use it!) They delve into your personal life with aplomb and directness, wanting to know if what you eat, drink, or wear is typical. They have asked about my lack of children and husband and have offered up fathers, brothers, and uncles as candidates.

"When living on the compound you are 'on call' for every crisis. Sickness, sorrow, and feud. I partake in all; inevitably the girls seek out the principal or myself. Needless to say, teaching is not my only responsibility. I run the dispensary, handling cases of malaria, filaria,

worms, footrot, tropical ulcers, wounds (from scratches
to the nearly severed toe of the cook and thumb of the
gardener, both self-inflicted) and the general classifica-
tion of aches and pains. I have sessions three times a day,
six days a week.

"Our compound has neither electricity nor water. Because of the lack of the former, I do all my work in the
daylight hours. In order to accomplish as much as possible, I have omitted the siesta hour. But rest is so vital
here with a heavy program that I gladly go to bed at 9:30
every evening. Being a city slicker, this was quite an
adaptation for me.

"Allow me to add here, that even though Owo is considered 'bush' or back country, I have never felt discom-
fort, never been ill nor indisposed. My house is newly
built, light, airy and comfortable. I anticipate running
water this month; but after managing on four gallons a
day, this is anti-climactic.

"I use mainly canned foods for the native market is
limited in its foodstuffs. Fruits, chickens, and eggs are
always available. I don't think we are expected to go
'Nigerian.' There are some things I like and some I do not.
No one cares one way or the other.

"The houses have the basic major furnishings: cup-
boards, tables, chairs, beds, stoves, maybe a fridge, bookcase, bath, or its equivalent. You are expected to supply
your own curtains, cushion covers, linens, china, flatware
and any other items whether they be decorative or not.
If you have the good fortune to be placed with an established volunteer, you have only to bring your own per-

37

sonal belongings. Otherwise you are expected to supply the other small furnishings.

"I hope to send pictures next of Owo, St. Catherine's, and my lovely girls. The school is new, six years old, relatively poor, with the basic teaching materials: books, paper, chalk, blackboards of black painted wood, maps, and library. Quite adequate.

"We have no science lab. Rough-hewn lidded desks and chairs fill the classroom.

"The girls come from all the regions and represent most of the dialects of Nigeria. The majority of fathers are farmers or laborers; the remainder have white collar or civil service jobs or maintain shops.

"Our staff numbers seven: two Europeans (the English principal and myself) and five Nigerians (one male). They are quiet and unassuming. I have made no attempt to impose my normally aggressive personality on them, but have moved gradually into their circle of friendship. We now banter and joke freely.

"The principal is a gem, a fine, kind, sympathetic, and understanding individual. She relates to the Nigerians with the right proportion of humor and seriousness. I feel fortunate in having such rapport with her and my colleagues.

"For those who have already taught, this teaching experience will not be different. You will encounter the same frustrations of lack of response or preparedness. It can border on the monotonous. A sense of humor in this case is a necessity, and a talent to innovate helps more. The difference lies in the fact you are in a completely different culture and in completely different surroundings. You become a learner, too.

"This information is a bit disjointed. I hope to convey as much to you as possible informally and realistically. Remember, these are *my* impressions and *my* views. Do not take them as generalizations! Other volunteers may have the same, and they may not."

Another teacher describes life with her students in the compound at the Centennial Secondary School, Sierra Leone, where she teaches Health Science, Chemistry and English. The only Peace Corps member teaching in a missionary school, she leads a quiet life.

"I live on the compound in what is called an African-styled house. My water for cooking and dishwashing is obtained from a tap outside. The toilet (flush) and shower are at the end of a series of four cubicles built outside of the living quarters. I have a kerosene refrigerator and stove, open shelves and a screened cupboard in the kitchen which would be fairly convenient if I had running water. We have electricity from 6:30 P.M. to 9:00 P.M. and in the morning from 6:00 to 7:00.

"Since I found carrying water, laundering, filling kerosene tanks, getting groceries, etc. from the village too much for me I have a man to do the chores. I pay him two dollars a week. He is a Muslim, speaks some English but cannot read it. We get along very well together. He comes from the village every morning, leaves at noon and comes back at four o'clock. He has the bad habit of borrowing ahead on his salary.

"We can get some supplies here—a limited variety of canned food, kerosene, cloth, thread, and toilet paper. Eggs at times are non-existent. I have had string beans recently in my garden and am hopefully nursing five carrots and some cabbage plants. We get oranges, grapefruit, papayas, coconuts, mangoes, bananas, plantains, and limes in season. Right now I am dependent on canned fruits obtained from Bo. There is a very good local spinach of which I have a good supply. Every Saturday a cow brought from the Fula country is butchered in Mattru, and Thomba is there at 6:30 A.M. to buy me two pounds. Occasionally I get a notice that a pig is being slaughtered and I buy a few pounds of pork. This meat is inspected in the village—I don't know how thoroughly.

"My activities are limited to the compound. The whites get together for an occasional picnic and I swim and play tennis with them sometimes. The Jong is a tidal river and safe for swimming. Sometimes the students swim with us. I do not get away from the compound much. I have no jeep, and the one school vehicle is in constant use for the business of the school. I have been to Bo three times and Freetown once. I can walk to the village but find it rather exhausting.

"The students visit me frequently and borrow magazines or games. Sometimes some of the girls help me make cookies. I have a constant stream of girls coming in to get weighed since I have a bathroom scale given by a departing missionary. They are as determined to lose weight as any American woman. And of course they seem to think a pill is the answer. I get quite a bit of nutritional information imparted in this indirect fashion. The girls are not

40

alone in their interest in weight. The workmen have just paraded in to get weighed.

"I am alone a great deal, since extra time of the missionaries is taken up with the four church activities. It is fortunate that reading is my favorite occupation.

"I was filled with apprehension when I heard that I was to be living on a mission compound. I was sure that I would never fit in. However, I couldn't have had a more congenial group to work with. I have only the greatest admiration for what they have accomplished."

Although relatively few Peace Corps volunteers are married, a fair number of couples—particularly such combinations as husband-teacher, wife-nurse, or husband-engineer, wife-teacher, have joined the Peace Corps, or have married after meeting one another in the Peace Corps.

This young couple writes of living conditions in Accra, Ghana, in a full report on keeping house for two:

"Marian and I live in a comfortable, three bedroom bungalow in the Kaneshie Estates district of Accra, about three miles to the city center and, therefore, a suburb comparable to Ardmore, Scarsdale, Lake Forest, Silver Spring, the San Fernando Valley. The house is on an unnamed street off Link Road, a main artery on which travels a fairly regular municipal bus line. We are about a quarter of a mile from a large market, a movie house, a bank and the main highway to Takoradi. The locale is comfortable middle-class. Our Ghanaian neighbors are accountants and oil company executives. All drive cars;

41

we are the lone family on the block without one (the Peace Corps refusing my request for a chassis, at least, to keep in the garage to maintain American prestige). The house is on a large corner lot which I allowed to continue growing to bush until Marian moved in. We hired a garden boy who cut the grass and now spends his time planting cannas, uprooting them and planting more.

"The combination living room-dining room is about twenty-five by fifteen feet and is fronted with a roomy stone verandah. Two of the sides are composed of eight eight-foot-high windows which permit a flood of sunlight during the day. We are on a slight rise. As we eat dinner, we can see the lights of the Accra business district twinkle below us. The floors are well lined with blocks of linoleum. A corridor extends thirty feet beyond the living room. Off the corridor are three bedrooms with large sliding door closets. To the left of the corridor is a tremendous family-style kitchen. Beyond the kitchen is a room for a cook. At the end of the corridor is a storage closet and separate water closet and bathrooms. A doctor, who is our landlord, lived here previously. The house is fully equipped. The toilet flushes. We have a bath and a shower (no hot water, which is rarely missed). The electricity never has failed. The kitchen has a steel sink and large work counter in addition to four closets for food and utensils. We have a small refrigerator (one and a half cubic feet) which I purchased for 30 pounds. We have a gas stove, complete with oven and four burners and a grill, operating on gas we buy in 32 pound metal bottles. The bungalow was furnished. In the living room, we have four armchairs and one two-cushion-wide sofa plus six small coffee tables and one large one. We keep a large stock of books in old wardrobe (slightly lopsided) in which I had shelves built. We have a dining table which seats six comfortably and six chairs. On it we have a small server in which we keep school materials. We keep a battery-operated shortwave radio, which Marian swindled out of an American couple in Kumasi. The cushions of the living room chairs are covered with cloth of various colors, selected by Marian.

"Our bedroom is fully furnished with a double bed, dresser and mirror, two chests of drawers. The single bed on which I slept before we were married is in a second bedroom with a cot I purchased to serve guests. The visiting schoolboys use these. We also made a six-foot table for them out of a closet door which had fallen off its hinge. The other bedroom is empty.

"The house is so situated that the sun never shines directly into it and breezes ventilate it constantly. I once thought I would need a fan. But we never have spent an uncomfortable night in the place. Air conditioning, which the three European families on the block have, would be a sheer waste, cutting off the fresh night breeze. The ceilings in all rooms are as high as 14 feet, making it hell to put in new light bulbs without a ladder, which we do not have.

"The house rents for thirty pounds a month. Marian and I pay five each. The school pays eight, the government twelve. I pay about a pound, eighteen shillings a month ($5.35) for electricity. A monthly gas bottle costs about two pounds, five shillings ($6.30). We always have

43

a spare bottle. We also are charged ten shillings a month water fee.

"I hired a cook and general factotum as soon as I went into the house (the school secretary helped me interview candidates at the government labor pool in Accra). With the usual difficulties of a newcomer, I probably could have muddled my way without help. In addition to giving an unemployed man a job and getting some of my wage back into Ghanaian hands, I find the cook a great help and time saver.

"His name is Hamidu, he is a Moslem from the north. He is illiterate and until Marian moved in with us, I had time to teach him a small bit of English reading. He speaks a pidgin, and we usually get his meaning, but we often have trouble reaching him. He cooks, serves, cleans, launders, markets, irons. He also is a fund of information about a part of Ghana life we ordinarily wouldn't see and know. He is about 31 years old. Hamidu lives in a room off the kitchen. He keeps a bed and a chair and table in the room.

"Combining two salaries, we earn 116 pounds a month. A budget may run, roughly, like this:

	pounds	shillings		pounds	shillings
Rent	10		Mail-postage	2	
Food (for two)	25		Magazine-papers	2	
Food (for guests)	5		Lunches	1	10
Gas	2	5	Bus-taxi fares	2	
Hamidu	12		Entertainment	4	
Garden boy	1	15	Books	5	
Electricity	1	18	Repairs (clothes,		
Pocket money			appliances)	2	
and misc.	14	12			
Savings (for			TOTAL: 116 pounds		
travel)	25				

44

"A recent sample Peace Corps budget for one listed 25 pounds for food. We find the total ample for two. We delight in Ghanaian diet, using Hamidu and the Ghana Nutrition and Cookery book as sources of recipes. Marian is particularly fond of *fufu*. For ten shillings, we bought our own *fufu* pounder. Ground nut stew is a particularly fine dish and much recommended with rice, *fufu* or boiled yam. We also enjoy palm nut soup, *konkonte* (a cassava root flour which has a consistency better than *fufu's*), *palaver* sauce (a stew or soup made of *nkontomire*, and the cocoyam leaf, which when cooked is extraordinarily like spinach). The soups and stews are made of meat or fish or chicken—sometimes two or three at the same time. We buy vegetables at the markets—green beans, brown beans, white beans and black beans, carrots (expensive), *nkontomire* (cheap), plantain and yam (both delicious when fried or boiled), and cassava root. A local staple Marian likes is *garri*, cheap and devoid of nutrition (as much of the Ghanaian diet is). Despite warnings and suspicions, we eat salad foods, lettuce, tomatoes, cucumbers, onions, okra, eggplant and radishes and experience no ill health. They are a part of the daily diet and much appreciated for the variety they lend meals. Fruits we enjoy in season: oranges and grapefruit year round, some of the sweetest pineapple we have ever tasted, papaya, mango, tangerines, limes, and avocado (if that is a fruit). We have eggs several times a week (they cost about sixpence each). Ghanaian bread is made with palm wine and is deliciously sweet, sometimes tastes better as it gets older. We buy meat, beef and liver, in the markets, grinding the tough beef into hamburger (make sure you supply yourself with a meat grinder). Fowl is cheap and tough, but tasty. (Tip: steam fowl 60 to 90 minutes before roasting.)

"Accra is well stocked with food stores. They have all canned goods (most of it's more expensive than such goods in the United States). Good cuts of meat are available in the department store cold stores. UTC, the Swiss outfit, offers fat sour pickles and sauerkraut. As for special diet tastes, Marian has produced red beet borscht and chopped liver for me. Hamidu probably is the only Moslem cook in all of West Africa to cook potato *lotkes* (pancakes)."

For many volunteers the hardships and the daily grind are compensated for in full measure by the excitement of new experiences, and in this case (Cayacayani, Bolivia) by the sheer beauty of the place:

"Cayacayani, the name and location of our vocational home, is my Shangri-La. Everyone has his own Shangri-La and I have found mine. Imagine if you will that you are taking a ride over a very rocky road when suddenly you come to a crest in a hill, and a breathtaking view of a lovely valley dotted with trees, small farms, and adobe homes unfolds before you. Then, winding down hill a short distance to a fairly substantial building, which was formerly a health resort, set in an unbelievably beautiful spot just five minutes from the small town of Sativenes.

"Mountains are all around you and the valley stretches out before you. Beyond the nearest stonehedge which is as near as your nextdoor neighbor back home you see our neighbors, the *campesinos,* tilling the land in the manner

46

of biblical times. Eucalyptus and pepper trees add to the beauty. All the varieties of cactus that you find in our Southwest thrive here and one variety which contains an oily substance is used as grease by the natives. Sheep, burros, cows, and hogs roam nearby. Women accompanied by small children are washing clothes outside our stone-hedge in a small stream.

"It is spring here and all the members of each family are out in the fields busily planting their crops. The men and boys using wooden plows while the women follow along sowing the seed. Tiny children are the onlookers, meanwhile learning the ways of their fathers. Throughout the countryside you can see women continuously spinning yarn on a hand spindle as they herd the sheep so as not to waste any time. They keep close watch on their herds and if one gets out of line they take aim with a rock which is swift and sure. Toward evening they can be seen slowly descending from the top of the hill winding their way homeward. The sheepherders may be women or small children who, besides tending their flock, have gathered firewood for home. It is a simple way of life but also a very hard one that makes them look old before their time. It is difficult to judge the age of the Indians as the young look younger and the old look older. Sanitation and nutrition leave very much to be desired, and this is the purpose for starting our vocational home.

"In the evenings we study constellations which are strange to us. We still haven't located the Southern Cross. A *campesino* told us it comes into view at four o'clock in the morning, so that would be reason enough. The stars are as bright as diamonds as there are no electric lights to diminish their brilliance. One can hardly do justice to the beauty of the nights at Cayacayani with native music, singing and laughter coming from a nearby field. This, then, is my Shangri-La."

CHAPTER IV

One Day
in Ethiopia

Rarely did a single letter from overseas capture the mood and the flavor of life in the Peace Corps as completely as this one from a volunteer serving in Ethiopia. Written by a young teacher, it is reprinted here in full:

"In the morning now when we awake it is raining. Our roof, as most roofs in Addis, is tin and it is pleasant to wake at six to the heavy, amplified rain overhead. There are shutters on the two windows of my bedroom that keep it dark. It is cold, too, and in the mornings there is dew in the garden. The house is quiet. Today is Friday—my day to get up early and chop wood for the hot water heater.

"My bedroom, like the other three, is big—twelve by twelve—with a high ceiling, a door out onto the front porch, wooden floor, dirty pale blue walls, and typical Peace

Corps furniture. The mattress sags, as a hammock, in the bed; the wooden clothes closet has a warped door; the desk is small and shakes. I have constructed an artless but usable bookcase of stolen red bricks and unpainted planks; the walls are decorated with maps: Ethiopia, Africa, the world.

"Chopping wood for the fire is a simple ten minute task; I do not feel like Robert Frost, however, and go at it dutifully. It is still raining and I work under a durable lean-to behind the house. My axe is a haphazard arrangement of wood and cast iron. We handle the weapon gingerly. The wood is eucalyptus. We buy it for 17 Ethiopian dollars a cord and stack it against a fence separating our house from the servant's quarters. A few days ago a baby baboon wandered into our compound. He sits watching me, an oversize rat clinging to the frame of the lean-to. I flip a chunk of wood at him and he scurries away, up the frame that holds our water tanks, onto the brick wall of the French School compound. I pick up the two handfuls of wood and return to the house.

"Once the fire has begun, the bathroom becomes the most pleasant room in the house: warm and quiet. I sit on the edge of our washtub relic and scan through a collection of papers and magazines that have settled, finally, in the john as fuel for the fire: old copies of the St. Louis *Post-Dispatch*; international editions of the *N. Y. Times*; the American Embassy *News Bulletins*; the Ethiopian *Herald*. Copies of the International *Time* we pass on to our students telling them to overlook the English, hoping they will gain some idea of what a free press is. Besides this there are copies of: *You and the Peace Corps*; *Ethiopian*

50

Tourist Pamphlet; Suggestions for Teachers Abroad (published by the American Bible Society); and a set of student papers on 'How I Spent the Christmas Vacation.'

"The water begins to boil; it simmers inside the tank. I go back to my room and pick up my shaving equipment to have the jump on the others. Alarms go off all over the house; they resound under the tin roof. Sam F____ is the first up, coming sleepily into the john. Tall, thin and blond, wrapped up in a blue Chinese-pattern bathrobe and looking strangely like someone left over from the Fitzgerald generation. He is usually very exuberant in the morning, but last night we were out late; he mumbles a good morning, stuffs some laundry into the basket, and shuffles back to his room in his Japanese sandals.

"Our houseboy comes into the house and hangs his coat behind the bathroom door; he bows slightly and says, '*tenayis tillin*' (hello) to me, then goes back across the dining room to the kitchen. We are without a cook at the present—our last walked out dramatically when we refused him a raise (the cook was paid $55 a month; the houseboy receives $35)—and our meals are a community effort. I finish up in the bathroom and go back to my room and dress. The whole house is up now. The room is still dark; I open the shutters—one overlooks the garden, the other the landlord's house; then I dress. We wear suits to school in Ethiopia which is not the case, say, in Nigeria where the Peace Corps volunteers have to dress in shorts and sandals to stand the humid climate. Here in Addis it never gets much warmer than a summer day in August, and then without much humidity. I then stuff a set of my 2E class exercise books into a TWA bag (these are used extensively by the Peace Corps volunteers for carrying the students' exercise books back and forth to class), check the schedule (today is easy, five classes), and go back into the kitchen.

"Jim P—— has already started the coffee and tea so I pull the frying pan out, cut a slice of Kenya butter into it, and hunt up some eggs. We usually are able to buy twenty eggs for $1—out of this, four or five might be bad. I break them into a cup before placing anything in the pan. Ernie F——, who is the only cook among us, crowds into the kitchen and I turn the eggs over to him and cut the bread. It is 7:45 when we all settle down to eat. Our meals are turbulent arrangements. The conversation is disorganized, amusing, loose. Breakfasts, for some reason, tend to involve spontaneous singing. We have three singers in the house. The tunes are mostly from shows, a primitive rhythm beat out on the tabletop. Lately it's parodies: 'How are Things in Dire Dawa?', or 'Why, Oh, Why Did I Ever Leave Massawa!'

"Classes start at 8:15 with flag raising and the morning prayer. My first period is free today so I linger over a third cup of tea and leave the house at 8:30 when everyone else is gone and the houseboy is washing up the dishes. Outside our compound the Churchill Road traffic is heavy —most businesses open at 9 o'clock. The immediate area in front of the gate is noisy with children from the French School. They are of all nationalities and range in age from seven to nineteen. The corner of our compound is a favorite unloading place. Tuition at the French School is $20 a month ($10 for Ethiopians). It is a highly regarded school and as a result draws the children from the embassies,

UN, foreign business. I therefore weave my way through the Cadillacs, Lincolns, Mercedes-Benzes. These cars are mostly owned by other than the American Embassy; the American ambassador's car is a Plymouth. The sidewalk conversation is also international, six-year-olds conversing simultaneously in Amharic, French, English, German. Seven languages are taught at the school. I pass through them quickly, cross the street and start down the hill toward the Commercial School. The weather has warmed up, almost 70 now.

"It is an eight-minute walk to school. On the way I'm bothered by twenty or so shoe-shine boys; a half-dozen boys selling the *Ethiopian Herald, Time, Newsweek* (they both sell for 75¢ a copy), *The Ethiopian Voice* (a Communist-leaning paper); five or six beggars; and a dozen taxis who slow down and call, '*yetnew?*' (where to?). At the bottom of the hill I stop and check our box at the Post Office, then cross the street again, walk past the Haile Selassie Theatre, and up Smuts Street to the school.

"The Commercial School is one of the three or four best schools in Ethiopia with five buildings, a large faculty, and 450 students. (The enrollment increased by two hundred in the last term when we took on students from Haile Selassie I School.) The three main buildings are grouped around a quadrangle, the fourth side is Smuts Street. Two smaller buildings are behind. The quadrangle is large and covered with stone; in the center is a small garden of flowers, the flag pole, and a bust of the Emperor. The buildings that surround it are grey, three stories high, and made of large bricks. Commercial School, as all schools in Ethiopia, was a boarding school until recently (this

53

year); the dormitories (two) were converted into class-rooms and a library, and, as a result, we now have a faculty room. The English faculty, having the largest single unit, was given a separate room for itself, and, after signing in on a sheet posted at the door, I go back to my desk and correct themes until 9:10—second period.

"My first two classes are with 2E. This is an experimental class. They are at a second year level, but have had one less year of schooling. The hope is that if the experiment works, education can be cut to eleven years, which would enable the country to produce more students, quicker. There are twenty-two boys in the class and two girls. They stand when I walk in and say *'Tenyais tillin,'* I answer the same, they ask *'Indeminadderu?'* (How did you spend the night?) to which I answer *'Dehna'* (Good, or very well). The class prefect has placed the yellow attendance card on my desk, and I count the heads and sign it.

"Today we're working on paraphrase—a difficult lesson in any language. More precisely, I'm trying to explain how we change rhetorical questions into direct sentences. I write a section of a poem on the board: 'But who hath seen her wave her hand? / Or at the casement seen her stand? / Or is she known in all the land, / The Lady of Shalott?' Then I write the paraphrase. The chalk is terrible; my hand is covered with dust. I slide out of my suit coat to keep it half-way clean and start again: 'But no one has ever seen her standing at the window, waving her hand; and no one in that district knows anything of the Lady of Shalott.' Hands begin going up. I call on Yohannes, who says he doesn't understand. 'What?' I ask him. 'Anything about paraphrases,' he answers. So I begin explaining every-

54

thing. It is a double period, and by the end of the first hour I'm back again where I started. Back to the *Lady of Shalott*. There are not quite as many empty faces, but yet they do not understand how questions can be converted into statements. I start another approach. 'Do you understand the poem itself?' 'No.' 'Do you have,' I ask, 'any poems in your language that ask a question but do not demand an answer?' They sit and think for a moment and then two or three volunteer poems. A few more faces light up. I turn to Ababayehu Asfaw, one of my best students. 'Can you translate the *Lady of Shalott* into Amharic?' He can and the class understands. Another battle won.

"At 10:35 I'm finished with third period and back in the staff room for tea—a fifteen minute break. These morning tea breaks usually constitute our English meeting. Today's discussion centers around how many official tests we should give third years. (Official tests are ones which count on the term grade.) This is easily solved and the topic turns to movies. *Splendor in the Grass* has just played and been thoroughly panned by the English set. Tom B——— is holding forth. He is chairman of the English section, about twenty-seven years old, small, thin, and having the appearance of always seeming undernourished. He speaks slowly and precisely, working his words over so that they come out well formed. 'You know he's got a good idea there, Kazan, but it's full of this Hollywood crap. Take for example the bit about his father. Why the way they carry on it's absolutely ridiculous! You know that's a curious thing about American literature—this obsession with the domineering father.' Muriel T——— speaks up. She is sitting crouched up on the chair (her favorite position), an

55

Edna St. Vincent Millay character whose voice is high and cockney. 'It's a bloody scream,' she begins, 'I think you Americans have been actually drenched in father-complexes.' She is still sitting in her foetal position. Leaning over, she lights a Players 3 cigarette and sort of shuffles around on the top of the chair. 'You can't write a bloody novel in your country without some reference to a terrible father, an unhappy childhood, a case-history of maladjustment. It's a bloody riot.' Tom speaks up. 'It wouldn't be bad if they could write about it in decent English. The only people you have that write English are Mailer and Styron, and no one reads Styron.' The debate continues; I try to throw it all back in their faces with remarks about the Angry Young Men. They heartily agree, which leaves me at a loss; then the bell rings. Eleven o'clock.

"I have the next two periods off, so spend another hour correcting papers. A long and tedious task: Examples from a composition by 10th grade students on a topic entitled 'Me.':

" 'I am interested in book-keeping, arithmetic and English but I am specially interested in politics and that is the reason which made me to smoke. . . .'

'It is interesting to know that I did not participate in any kind of school activities. I did not aware what the reason is . . .'

'After I finished school and get my diploma I will join in one company with a handsome salary. After I got money I will buy a car for my old father and mother. After I worked about four years I will marry

56

someone. Then I will go abroad for honimoun. After I came back I will have one child. . . .'

'Particularly most of the girls loved me because of my appearance. And some of the girls gave me a necked name called *Shegaw* means Handsome. After that all the teachers and the students called me Handsome, no on of them call Eshetu. Moreover that necked name went to town and the people started call me Handsome. . . .'

'Early from my childhood till now I do not like girls but I like boys in the schools. I disliked girls because they seem to me like Lucifer. The Holy Bible tells us that women were the first to led us from Heaven to Hale. If I got full of freedom of killing I may do my best. . . .'

'I am quite a good looking youngster of my age. My color is not black as negros and not white as white people of the world, but it is somewhat in the middle.'

"An hour is about all I can take so I walk out on the school compound and cross over to the woodshop. My students have been working on a bookcase and I've not been in to see them for three days; the bookcase looks as if it won't hold a paperback. I start to tear it apart but the bell rings for sixth period, the last period of the morning. I have 3B for comprehension. It's not a particularly bright class or interesting. Today they're having a test, a simple one, but it takes all period, they read slowly and frequently consult the dictionary.

"At one o'clock morning classes are finished and I start

57

back up to the house. It is quite warm now and the walk back is trying at this elevation. In the distance, up the slope of the mountain, is the center of Addis. From the Commercial School to the mountain is a three-thousand-foot elevation. The buildings are white above the clusters of eucalyptus trees. I stop at the Post Office Box and pick up the international edition of the *New York Times*. At the house, Ernie and Jim M—— have already put together a lunch of oxtail soup and tuna sandwiches. Table conversation is mostly about the morning classes, who is due in from the provinces, what we will eat that night. The conversation is seldom serious, but Sam has received a letter from a friend who wants to know if the Peace Corps experience is more valid to life than college. We toss the point around academically, never reaching any conclusions, but agreeing that, in terms of understanding anything about the world, the Peace Corps is an ideal training ground and that it keeps people away from the artificial world of college. As F—— says, seeing people begging on the streets and walking the dirt roads with leprosy and elephantiasis makes one aware of what really is important in life.

"The meal is over at two; we leave the dishes for the houseboy, and I go back into the bedroom and stretch out for forty-five minutes. I'm teaching Alan Paton's *Cry, the Beloved Country* this afternoon and am three chapters behind my students. I finish that off and turn to Lawrence's *Seven Pillars of Wisdom*, a book that I've been picking away at for three weeks. Lawrence is all involved with the cutting up of the Yarmuk Valley Railway and it looks as if he will never get out of the desert alive; I actually and acutely feel his frequent rounds with dysentery.

"There are only two classes in the afternoon. I return to school as the three o'clock bell sounds and climb up to the second floor to room 3C. They are reading Paton's book. I have this class ten times a week and enjoy it most of the time. Half of the class are girls, which is unusual, and of them three of four are the prettiest Ethiopian women I've seen. Students are still straggling in; a permanent habit of theirs, so I walk back and sit down next to Konjit Wolde-Rufael, a quiet princess of a girl. Her father is wealthy, as most of the girls' parents are, employed in one of the ministries and the owner of several coffee plantations. She is always impeccably dressed with her hair set and wearing dark glasses. Today she has on a pale blue dress with short sleeves and a low waist line. 'That's a pretty dress, Konjit,' I say, sitting down near her. She bows her head slightly. 'Thank you, Mr. C——.' Like most Ethiopian girls she speaks barely above a whisper. 'Did your mother buy it for you?' She replies by inhaling quickly, which means 'yes' to the Ethiopians. I imitate her and she laughs, 'Why do you make fun of me?' she asks. I reply that I'm not and do it again. She then questions me for a few minutes in Amharic, testing my skill: 'What are you doing this weekend? Do you have a girl friend? Why don't we go to the library and read instead of having English?' To all of this I answer lamely in halting Amharic. The class is alive with students chattering in Amharic; I clap my hands to remind them this is English and return to the front of the room. The next forty minutes we pore slowly over a dozen pages, stopping frequently to explain a word, a phrase, the general

59

meaning. The process has a way of destroying all the literature of Paton.

"Eighth period I'm back with 2E for a debate. Ethiopians are inherent debaters and they take to it readily. Last period on Friday is devoted to debates; today's topic is: 'Is Life In The Country Better Than Life In The City?' They could argue for weeks on this alone. A new chairman each week chooses the title and the participants. The debates are beneficial in that they force the students to think on their feet in English. At the end, three judges decide the winner on a system of points, the stress being placed on their command of English. Next week's topic, the new chairman, Asegedech Bzuneh, states, will be: 'Is It Better To Marry A Rich Girl Than A Pretty Girl?' I can hardly wait.

"When the bell rings at 4:30 I go back into the faculty room and straighten out matters for the weekend, collect the papers that have to be corrected, fill out another questionnaire from the Ministry of Education (I wonder if anyone reads them?) and sign out. I walk back to the woodshop and wave to Sam F―― who is out in the makeshift tennis court instructing three girls. In the woodshop I work with three students until six o'clock, then close up and walk over to the Ras Hotel for a beer with Jim P――. The sun has just about disappeared over the Debre Zeit mountains and clouds are moving slowly in to the north over Mount Entoto. We'll have rain tonight.

"The Ras Bar is not elaborate, but it is quiet and there is usually an interesting group of tourists and businessmen, passing through. It looks out on Churchill and the Caltex Gas Station. The Ted Shatto Safari's landrover is parked in

60

the driveway; a beautiful name for a big game hunter. Ted himself is sitting at the bar, a short, heavyset man with a small goatee for a beard. He is talking about hunting Mountain Nyala and Walia Ibex with a German couple who have green Ethiopian flight bags slung over their shoulders. Jim and I drink our St. George beer silently and listen. The woman, who is pale and blond, keeps saying she wants a greater Africa Kudu. We leave them discussing rifles and go back up home. It is seven o'clock and dark; the street lights are on up Churchill.

"Ernie is midway through preparing dinner and we give him a hand setting the table, cutting bread, making tea and coffee. Sam has located a cook through the American Embassy, so it looks as if this trouble will be off our hands. We settle down to dinner just as two girls from Debre Berham come in; they have been without water for a week and want to know if they can use the tub for a bath. We invite them for dinner and start the fire under the heater. By the time we finish dinner a dozen other province people have stopped in to use the phone or the john and check what is happening over the weekend. They all move on to the transient house where they'll spend the night. Landrovers and jeeps move in and out of the backyard. There is a temporary power failure in the city and we take the candles into the front room.

At eight o'clock two Ethiopian friends of ours, Tekie and Samuel, drop in to see if anyone wants to go to the cinema. We make more tea and debate the question; there are four shows in Addis and none start until 9:15. Sam has a date with an Italian girl he has just met; M—— is going to play bridge at the Imperial Turf Club;

61

P—— and F—— have dates with Peace Corps girls to attend a German Bach concert next door at the French School. (As you can see, life is difficult in the Peace Corps.) Teaching and the afternoon beers have left me weary, so I turn them down with a promise that we'll have them over within the week for 'injers' and 'wot', the Ethiopian dinner.

"Slowly the house settles down as the doors bang closed and everyone leaves; a few more telephone calls trying to track down province people. I gather the messages and place them on the marble mantel of the fireplace; in the morning they'll all be back at the house on their way up-town to do shopping for the week. Then I go out and chop wood for the fireplace and start a small fire. It has to be done carefully for the draft is bad. There are five sets of exercise books to correct but the weekend is long and I let them go. Picking up Lawrence again I settle down before the fire and get back to the desert. Lawrence has joined with Allenby to capture Maan, and outside in Addis it has begun to rain again on the tin roof."

CHAPTER V

"It Is
Hard Work..."

To most Americans the day-to-day activities of the Peace Corps remain a mystery. There is the general feeling that the Peace Corps volunteers have been sent to help backward peoples "raise their standard of living" or to "provide American technical know-how" for those nations that ask for Peace Corps contingents. But most of us would find it difficult to be much more specific.

Although this concept is not in error, the day-to-day job of volunteers is often far less grandiose than this. In the first place, the number of volunteers in any nation is so small as to have an extremely modest impact on its standard of living—no matter how tiny the nation.

Secondly, Peace Corps people more often find themselves working on the simplest of tasks—teaching reading and writing or helping to build a small school—rather than

63

explaining the intricacies of the gasoline engine or the generator for populations whose daily life is primitive, simple, and as yet untouched by the advances of an industrial civilization.

The majority of the volunteers find themselves teaching in the schools of the country to which they are assigned. Others are working as public health officers, nurses, and doctors. Still others are agricultural experts, or trained community development people whose first task is to gain the confidence of the native population, and then to discover just how the people of the country can achieve the rudiments of community life: a school, a hospital, a meeting place, a social structure, a road, or a warehouse for storing produce.

By this time, volunteers from our Peace Corps have accomplished small triumphs, working at the most intimate level with all manner of people in a bewildering number and variety of tasks.

In the letters that follow, the volunteers describe their accomplishments and their frustrations.

In Bo Town, Sierra Leone, a teacher takes time off while school is in recess to assist in the first national census of population:

"I am spending a month working for the government Census Department (there are five of us all together—Al A——, working with me in the Southern Province, Mike W——, in the Northern and Liz and Carl, in the East). Our job is to do a preliminary population survey of the major towns, mapping out enumeration areas of approximately 1000 people to assist the enumerators when they begin their work in April. It is quite a fascinating experience and is allowing Al and me the opportunity to get a good look at the Southern Province. We have already been to Bonthe and Pujehun, and after Bo (which may take a couple of weeks) we will probably finish up with Moyamba. Since this is, I think, the first census that Sierra Leone has ever had, it is presenting some difficulties. Maps, where they exist, are poor; the people, in some cases, are reluctant to give out information about size of family (because of the head tax); and sampling procedures are not standardized. We have worked out our own system, and that consists simply of taking what appears to be a valid sample of the households, finding the average number of people per dwelling, counting the dwellings, and multiplying. Pretty rough, to be sure, but accurate enough, I would imagine, for this stage of the process. The thing which makes it doubly confusing is that there is very little predictability about most of the factors involved. A very small house may have three families with a total of 15 people, a large house may have one family with only three people or another small house may have only one family but with about 30 children (multiple wives). All of which makes a statistician turn grey overnight! Oh, yes, in case you were wondering, we do have an interpreter with us (Mende in this case), and sometimes we get some of the local grammar school children to help out."

Meanwhile, in the Philippines, the summer vacation inspired a group of Peace Corps teachers to establish a day camp for Philippine children.

In the course of the summer they encountered a gang of
Philippine delinquents, locally known as "the Crossbones":

"I wished several times in my most tired moments
(which were every day) that you could have been there
to share what we had this past summer (Philippines summer). It's the kind of experience you don't receive on the
high, fast-living diplomatic level. You share in it vi-
cariously, though, through your camera, which I hope
will receive an extra hug from me when I take the film
in tomorrow to be developed. We four Tigaon nuts, Jo,
Gini, Claire and of course the only normal member of the
Peace Corps, conducted a summer day camp for out-of-
school children at Gini's beautiful beach *barrio*, Nato—not
on the grand scale that the Negros Camp Brotherhood
was, but nonetheless rewarding. Whether it was Claire
getting drowned by the kids as she tried to teach them a
simple swimming stroke, or Gini ogre-ishly portraying the
bad queen of 'Snow White and the Seven Dwarfs' during
story hour, or Jo tripping over her own feet in an attempt
to keep up with the girls in sports or dance, or perhaps
me the day I was writing the words to a new song on the
board—'No meat, nor drink, nor money have I none but
still I will be happy,' and one little genius to my back
piped up, 'Why?'—after which I picked my jaw up off
the floor and muddled my way on—or the day I finally received a smile from the saddest, most frightened little 12-
year-old boy I ever saw—who had never even seen the
inside of a school building before and was terrified of his
own shadow, let alone all the other children and those

four strange white monsters who must have seemed like ghosts moving about him.

"We worked. We worked awfully hard and never enjoyed work so much in our lives. You know the most rewarding time, though, really, was the night the sensitive-faced, punk, five-foot six-inch (19-year-old) kid with the spunk of a defensive mother lion and the brains of another Jose Rizal looked me straight in the eye and said, 'I never thought I'd see the day the Crossbones loved the Peace Corps, but you know, Sue, we all do.' The boy, Marco, is the ring leader of the toughest gang of delinquents in the region, and he and members of his gang made up the greatest percentage of our 20-odd teenage counselors for our camp. This tough guy was the tenderest, most gentle person with children you'd ever want to see, and our close association with the boys comprising our counselors resulted in an emotional bond of friendship that goes far beyond any normal relationship of the same or other societies. Marco and his gang of have-nots not only worked this summer instead of going out drinking and fighting, but they also worked side-by-side with a few of the rich Spanish, money-owning boys whose homes they had stoned in the past whenever the few rich families held their "exclusive" parties. Tigaon is infamous for its black-white issue, which is not a matter of color but is actually a political-economic issue. We became the confidants and big sisters of these boys (let alone peace makers), but they now rule our house—which is headquarters for one and all. It's been a two-way exchange and growth all the way. They, in their deep emotional bond to us, now sit us down and tell us all that is wrong with us or scold us when we commit a blunder. That's all I can say. I couldn't relate all the day-to-day incidents that went to make up this situation, but I'm sorry June is approaching and most of them will leave to return to school. I will leave and live in a house in my own little town of Sagnay, four kilometers away."

In Malaya, a group of American nurses and public health experts are at work under Peace Corps auspices. One of them describes the task, which seems to be bigger than the small group can handle:

"We are working in the rural health clinic, not the hospital. Two days a week we hold antenatal and child health clinics in Tapah at the M. Gandhi Hall. The other three days we travel to small towns, or *kampongs*, and hold clinics in a variety of buildings; these clinics also deal with antenatal care and child health. We give out simple medicines, give immunizations, and try to decide which cases should be referred to the hospital. On Saturday we visit as many homes as possible, but the need is so great that it is merely a drop in the bucket. We both feel that our greatest potential contribution is in home visiting, especially for the purpose of practical demonstration.

"More than half of our patients speak Cantonese, a few Tamil, and the rest speak Malay, which only adds to the problem. I have tried to learn a few Cantonese phrases, but Ruthie is holding her breath for fear I'll use the wrong intonations and get my face slapped!

"The health officer in this district must expect miracles

from us because on our first day in Tapah he took us to a *kampong* near Tapah Road and it was arranged that we would give a health talk to the women's institute this Wednesday night—in the Malay-medium, of course. We are scheduled for a repeat performance Friday night, at the Tapah community hall—that is after we wash off the tomatoes from the first."

One of the most realistic and poignant letters was written from Ethiopia. A volunteer describes how he and the other volunteers assigned to Ethiopia managed to set in motion a project that may "revolutionize student life in Ethiopia."
The letter is candid, hopeful, cautiously optimistic. The sense of pride and accomplishment shows clearly as the volunteer describes the close working relationship he and the others in Ethiopia have established with the local governor, the Ministry of Agriculture, the colleges, and the U.S. Department of Agriculture and the United Nations— all in behalf of a small secondary school in Wallega Province:

"It should be understood that I am teaching in the only secondary school in all of Wallega Province. This means that many of our students come seven or eight days 'by foots' (as they say) to reach this sole seat of learning. Coming from families that can provide little that resembles cash, they are almost wholly dependent on the small stipends that some of them receive from the government. A scanty few are fortunate enough to become lodged with relatives or friends, but the great majority must make their homes in the bars and cafes. Their diet is almost as poor as it is monotonous.

"In our moments of dreaming we set some goals: (1) to take the students out of their cramped quarters, where smoke and the noise vie for dominance, and provide accommodations more conducive to the pursuit of studies; (2) to set the students in front of three decent meals each day; and (3) to provide some productive outlet for their energies.

"Even when we emerged from our soft cocoon of dreams and faced realities, we saw some promise of success. We formulated a plan that was carried first to our school officials, later to our governor and to the various government ministries. A blueprint of our proposal would even reach the Emperor before the story was complete.

"On January 13, the Governor of Wallega Province, his Excellence, the Dejazmatch, Fekre Selassie Habtemariam, presented us with 13 acres of beautiful farm land just north of the village. Here we plan to take 24 students as a pilot project. To accomplish our goals and realize our dreams, we will build upon this land a combination of living quarters and a dining area that will incorporate study facilities and a library. Electricity will lengthen the days into the nights for the purposes of study and recreation.

"We have enlisted the aid of Ethiopia's two agricultural colleges, the Ethiopian Ministry of Agriculture, Point Four, the U.S. Department of Agriculture, and the United Nations to get technical data personnel to assist us with our farming program ... that we might attain a self-

70

sufficient basis while maintaining a demonstration farm for our neighbor and friend—the Ethiopian farmer.

"It is a project that we have lived closely with for a long time now. We have a wonderful feeling when we stand and survey *our* land. We are not trying to build memorials, but this is something that will last (hopefully) beyond our two-year tour of duty. Two years is a long time when viewed from certain angles, but it is only an instant when seen in the light of all that remains to be done here. We have a tremendous amount of work to do just to get our project off the ground, but it has many pleasing aspects for us. It gives us an opportunity to work with the students on a more intimate level than is possible inside the classroom. It is also bringing us much closer to the community in general. I have spent many hours this week visiting with neighboring farmers and arranging for them to come with their oxen and plows tomorrow and break the ground for us. We have also worked hard to get our seed-bed in. We will probably plant potatoes and corn now, plus our vegetables. These will have time to come in before the rainy season. There's not a real farmer in the whole bunch of us. We really have a lot to learn.

"Our great degree of optimism is youth's common weakness and asset. Our land contract reads 'ten years.' It will require ten years neither to fail nor to succeed. With a little effort we can fail overnight. But we look to more than moderate success before the end of our two years— to the development of sufficient momentum that the program can continue as long as there is a need for it. If we fail, we will have tried. If we succeed, we will have revolutionized student life in Ethiopia. It's worth a try."

One volunteer, working in Colombia, contrived a machine that would weave bamboo into a suitable building material. His simple device has been demonstrated throughout Colombia, and has made a real contribution to the economy and to the simplification of sanitation in this country.

Here, modestly enough, he describes his hopes for further application of the machine:

"Thank you so much for your letter of the seventh of September about my bamboo-weaving machine. As soon as I return to Cali (in about one week) I shall have some copies of the plans made up and sent to you and Mr. S—— of the Peace Corps, East Pakistan.

"Regarding latest projects with this machine, I can report the following: The head of the Public Health Department of the Department of Valle has approved a system I had presented to him which employs the use of woven mats of bamboo as a retaining wall for latrine holes. This new system will make possible a saving of around sixty pesos per latrine and will replace conventional systems of brick or concrete retaining walls. At present, a promotion campaign is underway by the Public Health Department to acquaint the people with this system, and my machine is being displayed in various areas of Valle in order to explain the process to the people.

"This system of using bamboo mats for retaining walls is not an unknown process here in Latin America. A Mr. Rodrequez, a Public Health officer who I have been working with on this project, had known through an OAS booklet that the system has already been very successful in

Uruguay, the only difference being that the mats were hand woven and rather expensive. With my machine they can now be made very rapidly and of a much better quality. He is presently in correspondence with the Public Health Department of Uruguay, and quite possibly my machine might be accepted for use in that country as well.

"Also, the Public Health Department of Valle has their engineering department considering other applications of the machine, such as cheap structures to house small animals, and the like. I am told that within a short time they will have assembled a brochure explaining its various uses.

"Regarding the use of the product as a building material for low-cost homes, I am still awaiting approval from Peace Corps, Washington, to proceed on construction of a large building which would serve to determine more accurately its cost in comparison with conventional systems and its general feasibility."

In Malaya, a volunteer who was assigned to teach machine shop practice discovered, to his consternation, that his students needed nothing more than some old-fashioned discipline:

"When I first arrived in Malaya, the thought of not measuring up to the expectations of these people here occurred to me, and I must admit that it was a little frightening. So I decided the best thing for me to do, in the beginning, was to go slow, and feel my way around by observing and learning from the people here just how

73

things were done and why. I soon learned how the things were done, but nobody seemed to know why they were done in this or that particular manner.

"I eventually came to the conclusion that things were done in a certain manner because this was the way they had been taught, and it had never occurred to them that there might be another and better way of getting things done. For example, during my learning period at the Technical Institute, I chatted with some of the fourth and fifth year apprentices of the Central Apprenticeship Scheme, and found that after being trained for four or five years these boys were not qualified to hold a job as a skilled tradesman. Surely, I thought, these boys are not stupid, and the instructors seem to know what they are doing, so there must be something wrong with the way the instructors are going about their business.

"I sat in on some of the theory classes as an observer and learned that these instructors were merely lecturing out of a book and most of everything they said was going over, around, or under the heads of the apprentices and very little, if any, was going through their heads. I suggested to the head of the apprenticeship program that I would like to have a class of my own, preferably first-year boys, to see if I could come up with a system of instruction that would help these boys to learn more and to better their chances of becoming skilled tradesmen. He gave the class to me and told me that I was free to do anything I wished, but he wanted me to keep him informed on the progress of the class, and, if I got some good results, we might have a class for the instructors.

"I started off my class by telling them who I was, why I was in Malaya, that I was going to be their instructor, that I was going to teach them machine shop theory, and that they were going to *learn* machine shop theory. I told them that if there was anybody in this class who was not there to learn that he was just wasting my time and his own. Believe me, I didn't know how they were going to take this sort of a start with me, but you will be amazed at what I am going to tell you now.

"I prepared a list of notes of the things I felt it was important for these boys to know, and had copies made, and gave each a copy of his own. I told them that I had spent a considerable amount of time preparing these notes and wanted them to study them at home. In the middle of the term I gave them an examination and found they just simply were not studying, because the highest ten scores out of a possible 100 percent went like this: 72, 70, 68, 66, 62, 62, 60, 60, and 56. As you can see, with a passing grade of 70, only two boys made the grade. I took steps to correct this situation by announcing in class that I was very disappointed in the results of the examination. I told them that I was very serious about this home study and that if I thought a boy failed his term examination because he was not studying at home I would personally recommend to the Chairman of the Central Apprenticeship Board that he be dropped from this program. These may seem like harsh words to you, but last Saturday morning they wrote their term examination and the ten highest scores went like this: 99, 96, 95, 95, 94, 92, 90, 89, 88, and 88—showing that these people can learn if

75

they think it is worthwhile. I found while observing the students here that they were very shy, and I do believe that my method has overcome this shyness, because I find that some of them are asking questions on their own, and I had one awful time getting them to ask questions when I first started out with them. The sum of my experiences at the Technical Institute, with the type of students they have there, adds up to this: they are able to learn and anxious to learn, but need to be shown how to learn."

Progress is slow, a fact that Peace Corps volunteers learn in nearly all countries in which they serve. Working with little in the way of equipment or supplies, with no large sums of aid money at their disposal, Peace Corps volunteers have accomplished small wonders.

The idea, so well expressed in this letter, again from Colombia, is "not trying to build things . . . but trying to build a spirit of self-reliance and self-respect in a people who have never developed this."

"Huila is a small and poor department, but the cooperation that we are receiving here from the government and private and social agencies has been overwhelming. I live in a rural school nucleus which is administered by the National Ministry of Education and has such forward-looking advantages as mixed classes, a school cafeteria, and a complete extension program. CARE has an extensive program here and has supplied the schools with sewing machines, agricultural hand tools, Cinva-Ram block-making machines, various school equipment kits, carpentry and masonry kits, and foodstuffs as dietary supplements.

"In one *vereda* when I arrived, the people were working on a school which, they had decided by community action, was a necessity. They were making a few blocks at a time, and at the rate they were going would have never finished. I suggested, after orienting myself to the local community and studying its problems and resources as I saw them, that they have a *minga* wherein everyone in the community would work one day and we could see faster progress. They accepted my suggestion, and in one day with men, women, and children working side by side we made about 1,000 bricks. They were pleased with what they had done, and we proceeded to have more of this type of community effort. In July, I was in the hospital with hepatitis and upon returning from a recuperation period, found that the community had decided, with the help of the extension team, to have a *minga* every Monday. There was a severe cement strike in the country which was followed by problems with transportation, so that for months we have been without cement. After a few days of hauling sand and rocks up and down hills and gullies by pure physical strength to the school site, we decided to build a road to the school—about three kilometers from existing roads—so that the dump truck from the municipal center could haul materials when they arrived. For three months now we have been carving a road out of the earth by hand. It is hard work, and one often wonders why they would do it, but for me the results are gratifying. It is almost finished, and we hope to start

77

again soon on the school. I hope that we are able to finish it by June, when my term of service is up, but if not and I hear of its being finished after I leave, by the very nature of Community Development, I will be all the more pleased because the community will be standing on its own and making its own decisions without an outsider's help. This is the ultimate goal of our work here, and I feel that the Peace Corps in Colombia will accomplish its task, although the results may not be seen for several years. We are not trying to build *things*, which makes the job difficult to evaluate, but trying to build a spirit of self-reliance and self-respect in a people who have never developed this and have always been done for and not given credit for being able to help themselves.

"Aside from the actual job, just the fact that I am here and that the simple *campesinos* of Colombia are seeing someone from the U.S. and developing friendships with him is important. I do feel, however, that I am gaining much more than they, in learning different customs, ideas, and manners of being. In this year and one-half away from the United States, I have developed a fuller view of life, a stronger pride in what our country stands for, a firmer belief in the necessity of a self-help form of foreign aid, and a deeper determination to serve my country further when I return."

In Nigeria, a young Peace Corps teacher, obviously exhilarated by his job, describes the close personal relationship that he has developed with his students, a relationship that perhaps will prove to be, in the long run, the most lasting of the accomplishments of the volunteers:

"It has been a long time since I have felt so thoroughly useful. My room in the University of Nigeria student hostel is overloaded with student essays for correction. I teach three classes, 70 students, freshman composition. You can imagine the complex experience this involves, since I deal directly with the writing and thinking of a new generation of potential intellectuals. Now my shins are very sore from some hard knocks I got in a game of field hockey with the university team. Touch football on a level, soft lawn is much less demanding than field hockey played on a hard, rough field with vigorous Nigerians! The water has been off all day today, so I am dirty and sweaty. The season is now hot and dry. Apart from the ups and downs of spirit with the work and weather, one thing has been constantly helpful to me, and that is the hospitality of the Nigerian people. It is true that some are suspicious, but they are definitely a minority. The villagers treat all of us with big smiles and real charity; I think that what suspicion there is dwells with the Nigerian intellectuals. But for the most part the students and other educated Nigerians have been very fine to us. I spent several days during the Christmas holiday in the home of a student who had invited me and another volunteer to visit him and attend a family wedding. I had dysentery afterwards, but the student is a good buddy now. Another student, a fine, sensitive young history student who will some day run for the Nigerian Parliament, talked with me in my room for four hours last evening. We are able to discuss any subject with complete openness, and I find this one of the most genuine relationships I have ever had. I think this young man will be one of

79

my closest friends for a lifetime. He has invited me to spend my summer leave with him in his home village, where he will teach. My major problem seems to be finding enough time and energy to do all that needs to be done and that I would like to do."

CHAPTER VI

The Vegetable Plan

*T*he Americans who serve in the Peace Corps have often despaired of ever having any measurable effect on the welfare of the people in whose countries they serve. Often, beset by administrative red tape, floundering in a miasma of uncertainty about their specific jobs, far from home, and on display in a suspicious land, their jobs must have seemed difficult to the point of being impossible.

Some of the quality of their search for a purpose, for a result, comes through in this long and detailed letter from Chile. Here, in concrete terms, one can see the development of a Peace Corps project from its idea stage through to its completion.

Reading this letter, one begins to see how the Peace Corps, through the imagination and idealism of its volunteers, may well turn out to be one of the most fruitful efforts at foreign aid that this nation has ever devised.

81

Certainly, this volunteer will never, as long as he lives, forget his struggle and his victory:

"For many Chileans who live in Santiago, our region is extremely remote. So it seemed to me when I first went there more than a year ago. Now it is the center of things, and I feel much more at home there than I do in Santiago. It could be that we are prejudiced, but we believe we work in the most beautiful part of Chile. The south of Chile, especially the area around Osorno and Valdivia is a region of rivers and small wooden bridges and of sprawling lakes with deep-blue waters and dark, rising edges of forest. It is rich in lumber, and there is any number of local craftsmen who work in wood, producing objects that remind one of the region itself. A number of Germans have settled there and have developed a very productive dairy industry, and these Germans frequently compare the south with Switzerland. Some help to complete the resemblance by building chalets on top of the green hills which form one scene with the mountains. We are never out of sight of the snow-capped Andes, and Volcano Osorno pops into view continually—even when you least expect it.

"Osorno is a lovely town where horses and wagons mingle with automobiles in the traffic, and horse-drawn coaches still compete with the taxis. The Plaza, or town square, is the prettiest I have seen in Chile, with a rotund concrete bandstand, a large pool, and walks that penetrate the Plaza from all sides to etch out harmonious figures when you look down on them from above. Osorno has just about everything—hotels, restaurants, movies, and fancy shops, and it was there that we came in the past year to revive our drooping spirits.

"Osorno is progressive as well as picturesque, and in both these aspects it is in contrast to Rio Negro, where there is still some unrepaired damage from the 1960 earthquake and a serious danger of unemployment for the workers who live in the shantytown alongside the government housing project where our headquarters were. The town's only industry, a flax industry, was destroyed in the earthquake. Rio Negro is a place which you can leave for a month, come back and ask 'what's new' and get stared at as if you were crazy. If you can't afford the time to travel to Osorno and want to let off steam, there is really no place to go.

"The biggest reason why Osorno and Rio Negro have ceased to appear remote for us is the circle of friends we have there. The care and kindness our friends afford us seem to be unlimited, and life with the Chileans is a lesson in good eating, good friendship, cordiality and gentility. They follow a more leisurely pace than we do and would interrupt the most important of work to express their fondness for a friend and serve him tea or wine. This is true of the richest and poorest of the Chileans, and I assume it is a characteristic of the Latin American culture. To the Latin, the most important thing in life is not his work but life itself and the series of human relationships which give it substance and meaning. I have learned a lot about life from my Chilean friends.

"Our team was sent to Rio Negro with the commission to select certain communities and raise their standard of living. The rest was up to us. We were without local supervision or material resources such as machinery or loans to entice the people to come to our meetings.

"Last March two Peace Corps men who were starting their work in another area were getting to know one community for the first time. They asked one lady what was the biggest problem they were going to find there. She responded dourly, 'Explaining to the people what you're doing here.' They, like us, gave their explanations during the course of the year; but this pressure to create explanations, to find a way to move forward with nothing but the resources of the people themselves, was exhausting.

"Although the months rushed by as our projects moved along slowly, we did accomplish something. The countless trips that Jan made in the jeep and on foot with a large, awkward flannelboard and a briefcase full of visual aids under her arm had the most intangible but perhaps most important effect of all. She concentrated on a certain number of *centros* and visited them almost weekly with cooking, health or nutrition advice. The work of the women in these sewing-circle type meetings under the direction of the *delegadas* was exhibited in Riachuelo, a small town west of Rio Negro, and was the talk of the town. Our promotion of cooperatives went well, and in three different areas we were able to get three or four communities to join together in plans for a regional cooperative. In all of these areas the people have made the preliminary legal transactions, had enthusiastic cooperative-education sessions and begun purchasing items collectively. In one area, Rupanco, we initiated a project designed to teach the people the possibility of producing and marketing on a cooperative basis.

84

"Rupanco is the site of the huge Hacienda Rupanco— one of the largest *fundos* in Chile with an extension of over 150,000 acres, where the families of two of the *delegados* who live with us in Rio Negro work as farm laborers. The now deserted *central* of the Institute was an old delapidated building loaned to us by the Hacienda. This was our headquarters in the area, and around an old wooden table in the kitchen of this rural school we discussed the project as it progressed through its various stages. The workers on the Hacienda live in seven sections, little clusters of houses and small workshops, spaced three to five miles apart. The cooperative was formed with laborers from six of the seven sections, and as we raced from one section to another we headed directly toward the Andes, with three volcanoes sometimes in open view until the road veered right and skirted along beautiful Lake Rupanco near the snow-capped mountains themselves.

"My role in the formation of the cooperative in Rupanco was a very small one. Among the 750 farm laborers there, many people had spoken of cooperatives before. Two had been formed but they were small, only slightly effective, and had lacked legal structure. I had been invited by a local schoolteacher to talk to the consumer cooperative she was forming among thirty members of the mothers' club in the school. There we encountered a problem of numbers. Legally speaking, a hundred people are needed to start a consumer cooperative in Chile.

"I took the problem to Don Tito Steffens in Valdivia— one of the leading authorities on cooperatives in the south of Chile. The solution he offered was logical but too sweeping for me to have dared imagine it. He advised me to form one large cooperative for the whole hacienda, and he offered to travel to Rupanco to implant the idea among the local leaders.

"The twenty-first of May was a holiday in Chile and the people were free to have meetings. This was the day Don Tito traveled to Rupanco. We assembled the people interested in the cooperative. There were schoolteachers, bosses, workers, and ourselves. Don Tito conversed for two hours with these community leaders, congratulating them on what they had accomplished so far and pointing out some of the defects of their former efforts. He convinced them that a cooperative made up of all the workers on the *fundo* was perfectly possible. The advantages were unquestionable, but there had been doubts as to the people's capacity to control democratically such a large business enterprise. For the sake of the laborers and of the movement itself, Don Tito encouraged us to try.

"The type of cooperative in discussion was a multi-activity one defined as a *cooperativa campesina* by the Chilean law. This can develop any kind of cooperative activity—distribution of consumer goods, savings, credit, housing construction, etc.—simply by stating it in its constitution. The two main interests in Rupanco were the purchase of groceries at a better price and the possibility of marketing their produce in Osorno.

"A cooperative that develops two different activities at the same time can become very complicated, and one schoolteacher suggested that they start teaching about cooperatives immediately. Don Tito agreed, but offered another suggestion as well—start with an experience in working together. This was my cue for the presentation of our project—*Plan Hortaliza* or 'the vegetable plan.'

"By this time the plan was not only my idea. Christian Valdivieso, director of the Rupanco *central* and a university graduate in agriculture, had taken an interest. He had supplied all the technical information while I studied the market and organized the details. It called for the participation of twenty members of the cooperative to plant two and a half acres of vegetables between them—each one planting one-fourth of an acre in his backyard. Although many of the details had already been worked out, we wanted to discuss the project with this committee of local leaders—especially with regard to the vegetables which should be planted. To facilitate the marketing process, a limited number was necessary. Carrots, lettuce, and cabbage were finally chosen.

"*Plan Hortaliza* was an instrument to teach the people to work together in a cooperative way. It was separate from the cooperative because as yet it had no legal right to buy or sell. Between May and December, these two ideas went their separate way. The initial group of community leaders, aided by a teacher from the Institute *central* and the local parish priest, began the campaign of explaining the cooperative to the workers on the hacienda who chose its name and elected a provisional directorate which began inscribing members. *Plan Hortaliza* followed a systematic schedule. By the end of June, Christian and I had found the twenty people whose fencing and soil were good enough to carry on the project. Then we began working together with the people in the care and planting of the gardens.

87

"Involved in the plan were many agricultural techniques to which the people were not accustomed. It called for the use of nitrate and superphosphate fertilizers, which they had hardly ever used before. The seeds were certified and from a reliable source. Weed killers were also used to test their effectiveness and a disinfectant designed to blot out a disease that had ruined almost everybody's cabbage crop the year before. Simple things like planting in rows at good distances apart and then thinning their crops were new to many of them.

"In almost midwinter we planted the seedbeds of cabbage and lettuce in the *central* and distributed the fertilizer and carrot seeds to the people. We gave our explanations to groups of five or six and in addition made countless visits to each garden during the spring: checking the seedings, reviewing difficulties, and spraying. In general the cooperation of the people was fantastic; they religiously followed the norms we set down. Only occasionally did they hesitate. The carrots came up so beautifully that they thought it was a shame to thin them and throw all those lovely plants away. One lady wouldn't let me near her carrots with the weed killer. Another kept the lettuce plants we gave her set aside until the moon was in the right stage for planting. But in the main they captured marvelously the idea of the experiment, worked very hard to prove it successful, and supplied information about the land and the climate which was indispensable to the project.

"Working with them was pleasant work, and our best tactic was to get the plump señoras giggling like schoolgirls (something which is not difficult to do) before giving them the bad news that they had to plant their lettuce farther apart than they wanted to. Because the men had only Sunday free for work in their gardens, we had to work on Sundays. This meant we'd hand out plants for transplanting when perhaps they had hoped to rest. One man, standing there with a bag of cabbage plants in his hand, put me in my place by asking me if I were a Christian. But this same gentleman, some two weeks later, after some rabbits had raided his cabbage patch, journeyed to Osorno to buy new plants so that 'Don Tomas' wouldn't see his garden looking so miserable.

"This was the kind of cooperation we received from the people. Mother Nature unfortunately cooperated less. In one section a frost wiped out the carrot crop. We seeded again. The lettuce seedbeds under our responsibility in the *central* produced much less than we needed. Uncle Sam saved the day with $20 to buy lettuce plants. In almost every garden the cutworm arrived and sometimes had destroyed more than half the cabbage before we got there with DDT mixed with bran to tempt and then annihilate this malicious monster. Fortunately, our cabbage seedbeds produced so well that we replaced every destroyed plant without extra cost.

"These events made for some very bad days in September, but the people placed their complete trust in us and never complained of the difficulties. They were experienced enough farmers to know that it hadn't been our fault.

"Our hopes rose with the new plants as they finally grew firmly in the ground. Soon in twenty different places in the Rupanco region there was a sizable, lush *chacra* of vegetables unmatched by anything that had been seen before. The project was already having a pedagogical effect on the neighbors as they asked their questions about the orderly rows of crops in three different shades of green. As everyone grew quite satisfied, I began to worry. I remembered how the mayor of Rio Negro had responded to me when I informed him of our plan by telling of a fellow *patron* in La Union who had produced thousands of vegetables and had been unable to sell them because of the tight grip which the large, year-round producers near Santiago have on the local markets. We had 20,000 head of cabbage, hundreds of thousands of carrots, and 40,000 heads of lettuce developing beautifully in the ground. I began to wonder how hungry the *pueblo* of Osorno was feeling those days.

"From the very beginning we had explained to the people that the project was an experiment. With regard to the disinfectants, the certified seeds, and the fertilizer, it had been successful. Now came the crucial moment in the whole experience—was it possible for the *campesinos* to compete on the local markets with the large producers in Santiago? They needed our help, at this more than at any other moment, and almost all the members of the Institute team rallied to spend some days in December helping them locate the market and devise marketing procedures.

"Our first sale was on the first of December. We packed 1500 head of lettuce in the Peace Corps jeep and the Institute station wagon at six in the morning. Though we had risen early the people rose earlier, and did all the harvesting in the early morning dew so that the lettuce would arrive as fresh as possible in Osorno. One person from each section went with us to help make the sale.

"Two o'clock that afternoon found us standing in the rain in the farmers' market in Osorno with very low spirits. Large quantities had been delivered to grocery stores at a good price, some had been sold at the farmer's market, and at least half of the lettuce was still sitting in the station wagon. Nobody bought in the afternoon, so there was nothing to do but send the discouraged people back to Rupanco. We took the lettuce to the Jesuits' home and went to a restaurant for a four o'clock brunch.

"We had learned a great deal that day. Although our lettuce was better and fresher than what was shipped down from the North, it was still too young and needed to form a better head. Also we discovered that it was easy to undersell the big producers. Their lettuce sold at 100 pesos a head on the local market. Because we paid little freight and no intermediaries commissions, we could sell at 50 pesos and still make a sizable profit. We also learned that the farmer's market in Osorno did not deserve the reputation of a 'producer-to-consumer' market but that intermediaries were buying the *campesinos'* crops at a pittance and selling at 100 percent profit. Consequently the public saw no more reason to buy there than anywhere else.

"While the rest of our group took in a Saturday evening movie in Osorno, Ken and I set out to deliver the lettuce to charitable organizations. Before we did, we made one final try at a sale. Earlier in the day I had grabbed a basket of lettuce and walked through a nearby shantytown. The reply from inside these box-like, windowless houses had been cordial but discouraging. 'Sorry,' they all said using the exact same expression, '*no hay plata*—there's no money here.' After hearing this for the *n*th time, I asked when there is money. 'Tonight,' they said, 'the boss arrives with his paycheck.'

" 'Perhaps the boss might want to buy some vegetables,' we thought as we pulled up to that same little settlement that evening. Ken sold from the jeep and warded off the tons of children who clamored around the curious sight of a gringo selling lettuce. I took one basket and started peddling through the streets. In five minutes the basket was empty. Three hours and two poor settlements later, we had sold all the lettuce we had been about to give away.

"This experience constituted the most important lesson of the day. We sold cheaply—three heads for 100 pesos. At this price we not only made a substantial profit for the *campesinos*, but we also made vegetables available to a poorer class of people who don't buy sufficient quantities of them at the market price. A whole new dimension was added to our work and we saw that it had a side effect —secondary but extremely satisfying. When the *campesinos* learn to produce for the local market, the poor people in town are supplied with better and less expensive goods.

"The other December sales went more smoothly as we put into practice what we had learned. Radio and press advertisement helped educate the people in Osorno of our presence in the farmers' market. The hour and date of the arrival of the train which brought the produce from the North was learned and our own sales were timed accordingly. Every trip meant the discovery of new possibilities for sales, and the people became more and more adept at taking advantage of the ones already established. When the people arrived a week before Christmas with the first carrots of the season, our vehicles were so swamped by clamoring housewives that we couldn't even unload them and with this, the matter of sales ceased to be a problem.

"By the time that half the vegetables had been sold, the plan was already a financial success. Among them they had made 600,000 pesos. Their original investment had been 7500 pesos apiece. When juxtaposed with the minimum daily wage for farm workers of 700 pesos, these profits represented a substantial increase in their yearly income. One woman told me she had paid her yearly taxes on her small farm alongside the Hacienda from the sale of her lettuce alone.

"Three days later they rented a truck for 15,000 pesos to carry the vegetables to Osorno, loaded it the evening before and cleared 150,000 pesos the following day in the market. What remained unsold they carried to a friend's house near the market, and two of them stayed over to sell the following day. As they rushed about their business, I began to feel like an extra-thumb; and when one señora picked up a huge bag of cabbage and walked by me as I was struggling with a smaller one, I decided I wasn't needed any more."

CHAPTER VII

Social Notes
from Everywhere . . .

*I*t is almost axiomatic that wherever three
or more Americans are gathered together, a newsletter or
some other informal publication will be established. It happened on remote islands in the Pacific during World War
II and in bomb-scarred fortresses in Italy.

The Peace Corps is no exception to the rule. Stationed
in twenty or thirty towns in one small country, unable to
communicate or travel easily, volunteers looked to news-
letters as a link between themselves and other volunteers
who were also hungry for news.

It was difficult to single out any one of the numerous
Peace Corps newspapers for inclusion here, but this one,
called Subsistence, seemed to contain a representative
sampling of news and gossip. It is published in Malaya,
and we reprint one month's news from various Peace
Corps outposts throughout that country:

94

"Jim W—— and I and three other teachers went with 40 students from the Commerce Club on an overnight trip to Dungun the other week to watch turtles. Didn't see a one—obviously they're afraid of foreigners. Donnie is planning a big beach party there in August for all potential East Coast visitors—can't guarantee the turtles, but a good time is promised. Perhaps Ruth will provide the dessert—home-baked, of course. All of us here are adding inches, attributed to too many samples of Ruth's specialties. Hate to make your mouths water, but her hot apple pie à la mode, cherry pie, cookies, and pineapple upsidedown cakes are among the best I've ever eaten, particularly since they're such a rare treat here.

"Teaching 28 periods a week is keeping me out of some mischief, but laughs are frequent. The other night as Jim and I were bicycling away from the Sisters' Hostel after enjoying one of Ruth's treats, I almost added a patient to the *rumah sakit*. A group of Malay workers were sitting along the road and, as I cycled by, one of them turned to continue staring at me. He lost his balance on his chair, and it landed on top of him as he went flying to the ground, much to the amusement of all.

"My first day in one Math class was devoted to a question session about the Peace Corps, my home and family, the space race, disarmament, etc. Finally, one shy boy in the back of the room raised his hand, and when I nodded he politely asked if he might ask a question. After being assured he could, he quietly said, 'Pardon me, but would you mind taking off your sunglasses?' I obliged, more than a little embarrassed.

"Another day I marched into the classroom, prepared

95

to impress the Science IV Chemistry students with a terrific lecture. After the usual 'Good Morning, Teacher' (which seemed unusually enthusiastic), I began a discussion of electrolysis. Dead silence. Looking over the class I spied many startled faces, none the least bit familiar. Blushing, I discovered that I was in the wrong classroom (Arts IV) and beat a hasty retreat. Needless to say, the room echoed with laughter.

"More tid-bits: Think Jim is setting records with his Honda, which arrived several weeks ago. Thus far, he's run out of gas three times and had two punctures. Also one casualty—me! I severely burned my leg on the exhaust pipe trying to get off the scooter while wearing a straight skirt. Hurried home to get out my trusty Peace Corps medical kit and after a half-hour of reading instructions, and searching for labels on the numerous bottles, applied some Furacin and a huge gauze bandage (designed to get sympathy). My roommate, Nee Aye, commented, 'I'm sure any victim would be dead before you'd find the proper treatment.' Anyway, I'll probably have a scar from Malaya to show my grandchildren—souvenir of a combat with *harimau* in the *hunta*, of course.

"PAHANG—Jean writes: Well, things have settled down to routine for me by now. I have a room to myself and share the hostel with six other girls. Two staff nurses are leaving the end of this month and one is coming back. All this shifting leaves us with a grand total of three staff nurses (including me). Of course we have assistant nurses, most of whom are very good, but still, for 120 patients that's pretty slim pickings!

"I've gotten along much better than I expected with no

other Peace Corps volunteers here at the hospital, but sure do wish at times for another nurse to hash things over with. The other nurses have been real friendly and helpful and are egging me on with my Malay and bicycle riding. So far I've had no run-ins with any pedestrians like Ruth did, but I have a feeling my friends kind of hold their breath when I ride. I feel steady enough, but I guess I don't look that way.

"Oh, yes, there are two other friends here. One is a small brown toad who spends his nights in the corner of my room and takes off again in the morning. I think I should start charging him rent. The other is a rat who also visits me nightly. I think he is trying to build a nest in my desk drawer, as he brings in weeds, seeds, etc. I'm trying to discourage this habit by dumping the stuff out in the morning, but he hasn't given up yet. Brother Rat also has a craving for soap, and leaves his trade mark (sharp teeth marks) in all four corners of the soap bar. He has also sampled some other goodies such as writing paper, tooth paste tube, and plastic bag, but he is a true gourmet and always goes back to the soap.

"EAST SIDE—WEST SIDE by Mark F___ and Bob R___, Malaya's intrepid travelers. The following information is based on eavesdropping, gossip, hearsay, and other sources of misinformation. Its relation to the truth is unknown. The East Coast news was gathered by Mark during a recent trip to visit turtles and other Peace Corps volunteers.

"MENTAKAB—Jean not only pedals her bicycle but also the organ at the local Methodist Church on Sundays. Visitors are always welcome.

97

"MARAN—Ernie (that clean-shaven rascal) just abounds in unusual stories. After an uncomfortable night he decided to show his young lovely Chinese *amah* the correct manner to make a bed. After a few movements in the bedroom she misunderstood his intent and immediately fled the scene. At last report she is in Singapore looking for a *decent* type. The gossips around Maran were just settling down when 'old Ern' planted two coconut palms in his front yard. Any Malayan knows that the only time one plants a coconut tree is just after one's wife gives birth. So Ernie has twins somewhere and the townsfolk are really proud of our versatile surveyor.

"KUANTAN—Arnie has joined Jim and Alan temporarily. They will all be moving shortly to different locations. Arnie has a mobile home of sorts being prepared for occupancy and will move to the Pekan area. Jim is being transferred to a hospital more equipped to utilize his talents, probably Ipoh. Alan will move to more modest quarters in Kuantan, yet to be located. Ralph and Jeanette, after just getting settled in their new flat, have reluctantly decided to return to the United States. They will probably leave Kuala Lumpur during the first week of September.

"KEMAMAN—Nancy expects to be transferred soon . . . location unknown.

"KUALA TRENGGANU—Jim W____ is fat and happy. His Honda sits in the garage with a flat tire and his comment is, 'I don't need it, *lah*.' His boxing class can be seen running down the road backwards and doing some of those strange exercises we learned. Jim recently dropped his guard at an inopportune moment and nearly lost a few teeth. Liz is doing a great job, according to Jim. She and John D. spent a night on the beach watching turtles (with other teachers, please). The teachers also made a trip to the fabulous Pulau Perhentian. It's a paradise of coral and tropical fish and, according to Cynthia, an occasional hammerhead shark. Ruth and Donnella are now enjoying the pleasure of the Sisters' Mess. Ruth is a fine cook and enjoys it. Jay and I recommend apple pie. Jim likes the cakes and cookies. Donnie was a participant in the recent sports meet at Kuala Trengganu. She didn't finish the sack race and was almost last in the three-legged race. We all enjoyed her efforts to prove her athletic prowess. Barbara completed her training at Pekan and returned to begin the yaws survey in Trengganu.

"BESUT—John D—— seems to be content with his situation. He is a bit off the beaten track but near a lovely beach and Malaya's finest rest house. It seems that John is not an enthusiastic cyclist, but after his fellow staff members read the *Time* article on the 'pedalling Americans' he was shamed into giving a short demonstration. He is still not enthusiastic. Carol W—— has been transferred to rural health in Segamat. While eating all that fish curry, she lost fifteen pounds and now is slim and trim (take note Ruth, Joyce, and Carol S.)

"KOTA BHARU—Such a happy group I have not seen lately. Pete and John T—— are content in their cozy nest although they won't win any prizes in interior decoration. Lois and Kay have settled down in the hostel and appear to be busy with their work. Ann and Mary are back at the hospital temporarily. They are observing deliveries and preparing for the new work at a rural clinic in Ulu Kelantan. They will be ideally located at Ayer Lanas, which is only 20-odd miles from Tanah Merah by laterite road. The clinic is entirely new and will be completed, hopefully, in a month or two. They and a midwife will be the entire staff. Cynthia and Jean spend their time mowing grass, raising chickens, and planting various crops. Cynthia is painting up a storm and doing some interesting things. Jean and another girl recently entertained the local classical music lovers. Yes, sir, dig the local culture! They also entertained a local housebreaker . . . an expensive evening was had by all.

"PASIE MAS—A small, attractive town accessible only by ferry or train. Didn't see Tom.

"SUNGEI GOLOK, THAILAND—A happy little community which has seen many Peace Corps volunteers.

"ALOR STAR—Rita and Jan find life at the nurses' hostel quite enjoyable. In fact, Rita finds it so enjoyable that she hasn't even ventured out on an extended bicycle trip while the other volunteers are rolling up mileage. Bill S—— recently found the attention of his students drifting from the point he was making in a lecture. It seems that his students found the sight of Verna walking by dressed in a sarong much more interesting than Bill's lecture on relative motion. Verna expects to move into the students' hostel soon, and visitors to the Rest House are certain to miss the sight of Verna in a *sarong kebaya*.

"IPOH—John and Arnie recently invited their sixth form students to their flat and a good time was had by all. John and Arnie both enjoyed the opportunity to answer the questions about America that the students raised freely outside the formality of the classroom. Arnie and John left Ipoh on August first on their pedalathon to Kota Bharu.

They were last sighted in Bentong and expected to reach Timerloh that evening.

"SLIM RIVER—The aroma of durian and curry in Slim River has been replaced by an odor reminiscent of old Italy. When hard-pressed to identify the fragrance wafting out of P.W.D. 129, infrequent visitors to Italy may be reminded of the canals of Venice, but they are quick to apologize when Joyce and Ruth serve up a steaming bowl of their specialty—spaghetti! Hungry travelers find it a hearty meal, and it is said to taste even better warmed over. Ruth is also gaining renown for her light-as-a-feather pancakes, each one endorsed by Aunt Jemima.

"KULIM—Carole is in the market for a rifle guaranteed to stop a boar. She expects to take a trek into the jungle soon in search of them wild 'beasties.' Not to be outdone by all of this is Jane, who is sharpening up her tennis eye and, bedecked in her tennis outfit, should stop something.

"KOTA BHARU—Pete Kramer writes: Lois E____ is working the day shift in a male ward and is living in the rather plush accommodations of the nurses' hostel. John T____ is living with me and has just returned from a disastrous excursion to Besut. He, Lois and Tom J____ were visiting down there and now look like Indians (American variety). John is teaching at Sultan Ismail College with me. His subjects are chemistry and physics. Although fairly content, he would rather be teaching more advanced pupils. This opportunity will arise shortly when the H. M. leaves.

"Mary and Ann are still in Jitra and are missed terribly by their brethren here. Cynthia and Jean are now com-

Please do not turn down the corners of the pages. Use a book mark.

pletely settled in their new house. Every day one of them can be found mowing the lawn, weeding the garden, watering the plants, or draining the swimming pool. Although it pains me to admit it, their house is on the verge of becoming as liveable as mine. But they'll never top my cook! Jean seems to be spending long hours fighting the Dewey Decimal System for her school library. The remainder of her time is invested in stargazing. She can now identify 3,962,011 constellations blindfolded. When not laboratorizing, Cynthia can usually be found painting or scrabblizing with Carol W——. Cynthia's pet cat has disappeared. I have just returned from the Kelantan primary school combined sports competition, where, in all modesty, I did an outstanding job of judging the girls' long jump.

"I'm now playing golf a few times weekly, but aside from that, my life is quite routine.

"Tom J—— is posted in Pasir Mas and last weekend came in for a visit along with John B—— from Besut. A Malay friend of mine just returned from a trip to the States. While there he visited with Mary's and my parents. We spent a few days last week in the company of a few of the Dewan Latehan Rida students from Kota Bharu."

CHAPTER VIII

"An Experience
You Will
Never Forget. . ."

*I*t *didn't take long for the first group of
Peace Corps volunteers to become "old hands" at the job.
Their experience as the first volunteers was, by definition,
a pioneering adventure. As the Peace Corps began to re-
cruit and train more volunteers, these pioneers became the
only source of first-hand information about a variety of
things that the new recruits wanted to know about.*

*Most of the letters that follow were written in answer to
a specific request, either from Peace Corps headquarters
or from new volunteers who were about to be sent overseas.*

*The advice that is given ranges over every subject—
feminine fashions, dating, what kind of books to take,
native reactions to volunteers, racial segregation, and the*

hardships and the boredom that often overtake the volunteer during his two-year stint in the Peace Corps.

The first letter is from an American engineer in Tanganyika:

"I feel my personal working experiences cannot be of much help, but I hope a few of my general feelings and impressions can be of use.

"1. In participating in the Peace Corps one should consider two sides of every man's life. The historical side, where one moves within the framework of the big overall picture (Tolstoy's 'one's elemental life as a unit in the human swarm') and the personal side, where one works within the framework of his own interests and peculiarities. Taking one's place in the Peace Corps is a conscious effort to make a significant contribution historically. This idea will often be a source of satisfaction to you.

"But I feel that life is basically a very personal thing, and the historical motivation is not always sufficient to sustain oneself unless you are one who can constantly derive energy and meaning from causes outside yourself. Where one experienced historical frustration in America, one is likely to experience personal frustration out here. For me this personal frustration has taken two forms: (1) The feeling that I could better pursue my interests in engineering (or whatever one's interests may be) doing higher standards of work in America. (2) The absence of love (for want of a better word) or the prospect of finding it. For me this has been the personal sacrifice of joining the Peace Corps. Be prepared to make one.

"2. For those living in the large towns the physical

adjustment will be negligible. I am located in the bush and finding the adjustment no hardship. The Indian and Arab merchants supply anything and everything wherever you want it.

"3. Like segregation in America, colonialism has left its multiple problems in interracial relations. You are going to be grouped as a European and expatriate as soon as you arrive. There have been white nurses, engineers, teachers, agricultural and community development workers in Africa for years. Your living quarters are most likely to be located in European sections. You'll be invited out constantly by Europeans, and you'll more than likely accept. The extent to which you try to set yourself apart from the European community will be entirely up to you. Moving in African circles (I hope because you sincerely want to and not just to draw attention to yourself—which I fear has too often been my motivation) will require your really bearing down on the language and being prepared to face suspicion from both the Europeans and Africans. I have found the effort well worthwhile.

"With regard to social justice, the world is burdened by the mistakes of the past. The Peace Corps is an opportunity to try to correct them—but don't forget the realities of human nature.

"4. Contributions through activities other than my work have come through teaching English classes at night and helping form a soccer team among the workmen (we haven't won a game).

"My close contacts have been with the English-speaking Africans (engineering assistants, teachers, medical officers, government clerks). Having friends over to one's home for dinner is always a nice gesture. Attend local events and don't be afraid to participate in dances, sporting events, dramatic groups, etc.

"5. While you are not shackled by demands of rigid behavior and duty, you also don't have the satisfaction of meeting an always well-defined goal and purpose. You are very much on your own.

"6. Do not fall before the temptation of categorizing or generalizing, especially when you first arrive. People are people and life is life no matter where one lives. You will find your good and bad people regardless of race, and you will have your good and bad moments.

"That's about it—my best wishes to you."

The writer of this letter does his best to paint a balanced picture of what the new volunteer can expect in Colombia. His eloquence is matched only by his practicality:

"In general, life for the volunteer in Colombia is an unforgettable experience. You will encounter some serious changes, and it is not in the first month or two that these will affect you but after you have lived with them for a while. This is because everything is new and different at first, but as the newness wears off the monotony begins to set in. At first, you will find it rather tiresome to have to speak Spanish all day long. The people are different but very friendly, and you aren't sure where you stand in the community. Later, the bugs and the food start to get to you. Food here is not like the Latin American food that you get in the States. It is bland, tasteless, and the same thing day after day. The principal foods in the village are rice, yucca, plantano, potatoes and tough meat. You will no doubt experience fleas, cinch bugs, gnats and flies. At times you will think that every bug that bites, stings, chews, flies, crawls, or walks can be found in Colombia. When you visit the house of the *campesino* you will find the country different and beautiful. You will have many interesting talks comparing Colombian life with that in the U.S. After a time, you will be welcomed warmly into the homes of the villagers, and you will find that you enjoy sitting down to a plate of chicken or *cuy* (guinea pig) and talking about the problems of the people as you eat. There will be many little heartwarming incidents in which the people do or say something that will make you feel that your problems are very minor. You will experience the joy of the people upon completion of a road or an aqueduct that the people had been trying for twenty years to build. All in all, it will be an experience that you will never forget and will enjoy reviewing and seeing whether you did a worthy job.

"Following is a list of things that you should bring from the U.S.: Pipe Tobacco—If you don't smoke you won't have any trouble in disposing of it. American cigarettes are to be obtained here. Levis—These are difficult to get here and they are very useful. Sunglasses—If you wear glasses I would suggest that you get a pair of prescription glasses. Otherwise a good pair of polaroid sunglasses as the sun is very strong. Tie—You cannot get a decent tie here. Camera —Film can be bought here. It takes a month to develop Kodachrome, but Ektachrome, Agfacolor, Kodacolor, and black and white can be developed rather fast. The processing here is of poor quality. Razor Blades, Shave Lather,

Deodorant—They can be bought here but are of poor quality. Shoes—If you wear larger than a size 9 you will have problems in getting shoes. Musical instruments, pocket novels or hobby equipment that are easy to transport. You need not bring a supply of medicinals, clothes, socks, etc. at these can be bought here for the same prices that you pay in the U.S.

"I hope that this gives you a little picture of our life in Colombia. It's hard to know just where to begin or what to say. One thing I can say is good luck."

If there is one question that bothers any new volunteer, it is, "How will I get along with the people?" In each Peace Corps post, the reaction differs—but by and large the word from the first volunteers is cheering. Although a good many volunteers were looked at with suspicion and hostility, most of them managed to overcome the initial frostiness and develop a friendship with the people they worked with:

"What is the reaction of different groups to the Peace Corps volunteers? The students tend to be very much in favor of the volunteers. I have heard of no instances of trouble with anti-American students. On the contrary, they try to emulate you in every way possible. This may manifest itself in a broad American accent, or in an attempt to copy the teacher's mannerisms. They are also interested in any and all things American. American music is extremely popular, especially rock and roll and the twist.

"The great majority of Ghanaians also show a great liking for the Americans. I leave the newspapers out of this, because the two party newspapers, the *Evening News* (C.P.P. paper) and the *Ghana Times* (official government paper), tend to take a neutral to pro-Eastern stand on most matters. However, you will find, I think, a great well of good feeling for us here. I must say that the Peace Corps has not hurt this feeling. It certainly has not hurt for us to know some of the Twi language.

"The knowledge of their language has a profound effect on the villagers. You don't have to know too much, but if you have the proper answer to a greeting, it raises your prestige a great deal. They will laugh at you but they are proud that you are making the attempt to speak their language. Oh yes, the proper answer to '*Broni*' when it is yelled at you, is '*Bibini.*' This seems to make a big hit, in my area anyway.

"As for the British and American communities in Ghana, for the most part you will find them to be very friendly and helpful people. Of course, there is bound to be the individual who makes your hackles rise. There is one Englishman who makes me angry every time I see him, but he has the same effect on the British, so I am not too worried. You will find that this type of person is in a distinct minority. The British tend to be a little distrustful of most Americans, because they tend to raise the cost of living by paying exorbitant prices to workers and traders. This cannot be said of the volunteers, though, as we don't get the salaries other Americans do and have to watch our money fairly carefully.

"The Americans have been willing to give us any help we may desire. They are generally a pleasant bunch of people, again with the occasional exception to the rule, and will bend over backwards to make you comfortable. The only people who are hard to get to know are the Russians. There are a great many here, and more are coming. At present, most of them are up north, or in Accra. They travel in groups and talk little, if at all, with anyone outside the group. They are the closest thing I have seen to the so-called Ugly American image.

"They are even somber when they go to the Lido. The Lido is a local nightspot which has a bad reputation as a place for pickups. Naturally, this is where all the Peace Corps volunteers go for an evening of high life. Actually, they have a fine band, and the drinks are not too expensive. A few other places that are nice to go for drinks and good food are the Star Hotel and the Ambassador. The Glamour gives you fine Indian curry, while the Casanova gives you belly-dancers with your meal.

"The biggest dance here is the 'high-life.' Everyone who comes here must learn it. It is akin to West Indian Calypso and entails a mass of bodies shuffling around a cement dance floor. It ruins shoes, but it is fun. If you like, you may learn classical high-life but if you are like me, you learn bush high-life. This is a no-holds-barred type of dance, where you may use any step you like, as long as you remain relatively in step and don't knock anyone down. Oh yes, we also have the twist here. The Ghanaians do it very well, as do most volunteers. Typically, I managed to hurt myself doing the twist, but that will come under the medical section, so I shan't say anymore along that line here.

"An essential in the world of male fashions is khaki trousers. They can stand heavy washing and do not fall apart easily; I wear khaki every day, in school, as do most other volunteers. Shorts, also, will be of value in this climate. However, it should be noted that in areas such as mine sand-flies take a toll of those who wear shorts. Another item of value is the long-sleeved white shirt. It may be used for formal dress and helps to keep the mosquitoes off your arms. Sandals, too, are used a great deal out here. Along with these, you might bring a good pair of tennis shoes or sneakers (the brands sold here are inferior and fall apart in a few weeks) and rain boots, which prove to be a necessity if you are in a very rainy area.

"I almost forgot, you ought to bring out a wash-and-wear suit or two. You go out enough to warrant the wearing of suits, but any clothing that needs dry-cleaning is bound to be a waste. You should not expect to be able to have anything dry-cleaned in Ghana. The last time I saw dry-cleaning was at the American Trade Fair, in Accra.

"As far as toilet articles are concerned, men can get anything they want here. This is probably because we tend to be less choosy. I had to switch from one brand of toothpaste to another, but managed the transition without too much difficulty. Girls, on the other hand, find it hard to get the shampoos, home permanents, and makeup they like, so I would advise bringing a good supply with you if you are fussy.

"Books are next on my list. If you can, badger the Peace Corps officials until they give you a good idea of what you are going to teach. We had no idea, and had to spread our libraries out pretty thinly, trying to prepare for any contingency. If they don't tell you, then you can only follow our example. That is, a general library with a strong emphasis on fields you may be called upon to teach.

"My library falls into certain major categories. There are books on African history, British and American literature, geography, American and European history, philosophy, and assorted books on English grammar and structure. A good solid dictionary will also prove to be helpful. I might add, here, that the book store at Legon is a fine one, and the books are not expensive at all.

"For those of you who think you are escaping the nine-to-five grind; you are! You work from seven to two. Life does not change as much as you think it will. You are doing a job that requires that you do the same type of work, day after day, through the months that you are here. Life will not be very exotic after the first excitement wears off. There will be the occasional exciting events, but it runs about the same at home.

"Looking back over the last eight months, I find that my taste has dulled considerably. Movies that I wouldn't be caught dead seeing in the States help to kill an evening once a week. You also lose contact with all the new trends in books, plays, etc. Then there are the women. In eight months I have seen some remarkable changes in the expatriate and African women nearby. They seem to change for the better every month.

"Before I start crying over the typewriter, though, I will move on to the running of your home. If you live alone, in a Ghana Trust house, life is not bad. My house has two bedrooms, a living room, dining room, den, kitchen, bathroom, and toilet.

"As far as running the house is concerned, mine seems to run itself. My pay covers the electric bill, water bill, conservancy fees, rent, and a few nonessential luxuries such as food and tobacco. Clothing is no great problem and doesn't cost a great deal. Medical fees are virtually non-existent.

"This leads into the matter of health in Ghana. With all the shots you will be getting, you will probably think that you are entering the nearest thing to the Black Hole of Calcutta. This just does not prove true. I have heard of very few volunteers who have been very sick. Of course, you have your cases of malaria, dengue fever, dysentery, and sand fly fever, but strict adherence to the major rules will make life relatively illness-free.

"If you do get sick, Bill C——, the Peace Corps doctor, usually has the remedy. If he doesn't, he at least smiles as he tells you. Seriously, there have been only a few things that have warranted any real notice. One fellow came down with hepatitis—he drank bad water—and was hospitalized for a while; and I have the distinction of having the Ghana Peace Corps' first and second operations. The first one removed a cyst, and the second patched me up after I tore myself open again doing the twist in the Lido."

Any Peace Corps girl headed for Ghana got an earful of advice and information on matters feminine from this pioneer, who explains in detail what life will be like on two most important matters so dear to the feminine heart —men and clothes. This letter, incidentally, is from one of the girls who found her husband in the Peace Corps.

"I think American girls coming to Ghana need special briefing about social life and dating. Everywhere dating is the most natural way for a single girl to go places, make

113

friends and get around. This is as true in Ghana as anywhere else.

"Sex in Ghana is extremely casual. A Ghanaian boy and girl who attract each other will naturally go to bed together, without its meaning obligations, deep feelings, or scoring conquests. They won't think anything of having sex relations their first time out together. People live together casually. The only thing that is considered abnormal is for a person to live alone.

"So, a Ghanaian man who asks an American girl to go out has not had two months' training or orientation course on American mores. Most likely he will expect her to be like the girls he has grown up with, the other girls he has known. He'll make a proposition and she, though she may not admit it, will be insulted and scared. Three bets she will ask to be taken home and will certainly not go out of her way to see him again. On his side, he probably will think she is a cold, unapproachable sort who is prejudiced against Negroes and against him in particular.

"I am not suggesting any girl change her morals. But she must loosen up to the extent of realizing that sexual advances aren't meant as any insult, offense, or slight to her character—far from it! She really is doing herself and the fellow an injustice if she doesn't sympathetically explain the differences between American and Ghanaian customs. And this may take some conversation, since the Ghanaian probably has studied no American sociology (though some Ghanaians know that whites differ in this respect).

"The whole thing is less of an issue to the Ghanaian (unless he thinks race prejudice is involved). Once he understands, he is likely to have it the girl's way and pursue the friendship, which was what interested him in the first place.

"The white community has an astronomical proportion of single men to single women. When I was in Kumasi, I believe the word was that there were several thousand men to seven single women in the Ashanti region! This makes it easier, of course, to slip into white rather than Ghanaian circles. In towns it's pretty true that anywhere a single girl walks there is a white or Lebanese man who offers to drive her there, to pick up the tab on drinks, food, etc. . . . Social life for single girls in Ghana can be very interesting and lively, though I myself was ready to leave the whirl and get married.

"I had no clear idea how women should dress in Ghana before I arrived. I discovered that it's a very individual matter. There simply is no one group or society of people with a group standard for you to follow. On the street you see women in Ghanaian dress, women in Western dress of any style or description the wearer happens to fancy, or have left over, and women in Indian saris. You are stared at anyway because you are white, but so long as you are in Western dress no attention is paid to its material or the length of your skirt, or the shoes you wear.

"Some Ghanaian and some 'European' women are extremely stylish dressers. In fact, Accra, in Nigerian novels and other references, has the reputation of being the Paris of West Africa. The Accra girl and Accra cloth set the standard. We have visited three other West African capitals—Lagos, Monrovia, and Freetown—and nowhere did we see women with the same chic, girls with the same sophisticated flair for clothes and makeup that we see in Accra.

Every upperclass Ghanaian girl has a collection of what I would consider cocktail dresses in bright colored prints and vividly lovely materials. She wears these on the street, but not so often as workaday or dressy Ghanaian clothes, of which she also has an ample wardrobe. She never wears nylons, in fact no one wears nylons. The two Ghanaian women who teach at O'Reilly often come dressed in what I would consider party dress. Other days they wear a simple cotton skirt and blouse. At a nightclub, on the other hand, you sometimes see women very simply dressed.

"These Ghanaian standards of dress don't apply to us. In expatriate groups, English dress as they always do, French and Americans the same, but it doesn't mean much.

"Wherever you are going to be stationed, you should pack for a two years' camping trip—a two years' moratorium on the social importance of clothes. You should certainly bring with you a two years' supply of your favorite underwear and sleeping wear. The three department stores and various Lebanese stores carry these things, but it's very unlikely they will have your brand. Light-weight summer dresses, skirts and blouses are useful and indispensable if you have to rush immediately up country. In Kumasi, Accra, Cape Coast, Taworadi—any fair-sized town— thorough, skilled seamstresses will make clothes for you at a low cost. A seamstress in Kumasi made my wedding dress in November, a cocktail-length white taffeta with gold lace trim which came to about $25, including workmanship and materials. Mrs. Comfort Laryea and her twelve girl apprentices in a little shop near O'Reilly School recently made me a simple skirt for nine shillings and sixpence ($1.35). Including the cost of material at five shillings a yard, the skirt cost about $3.50! I highly recommend having clothes made here. Ghanaian stores have a wider range of lovely materials than I have ever seen before, including distinctive wax print cloths with proverb names such as 'poor no friend,' depicting folk themes in flowers and birds and arabesque patterns. An article in a recent issue of *West Africa* commented disapprovingly on the large stockpiles of cloth and the unnecessary amount of money spent on cloth in Ghana when it should be spent developing the economy. It also may be your only chance of a lifetime to have your own seamstress at a low cost and order custom made clothes in any style you desire (and can explain to the seamstress).

"I also had a Ghanaian dress made by the Kumasi seamstress for a total of $10. The Ghanaian dress with ankle-length wrap-around skirt and stole requires a full eight yards of material for which I chose a rather expensive plum-colored flower print. Aside from another Peace Corps girl, I have not seen another white woman wearing Ghanaian dress. I have worn it in Kumasi and in Accra. It takes some courage to go out in it because it causes a favorable sensation. A white woman is conspicuous enough anyway. Each time I wear it people wave and call out, and strangers invariably comment. When I wore it to lunch at the Government Rens House in Kumasi (where Peace Corps teachers of the area have formed a pernicious habit of clubbing Saturday afternoon) a waiter came and asked for my photograph. When I wore it to the YWCA restaurant in Accra the cab driver as we got out asked Arnold, 'white woman, or black,' and answered his own question, 'I think be black woman.' He was serious, which was truly surprising since I have fair, orange-blond hair. I recommend getting at least one Ghanaian dress. I know I'll enjoy taking mine home with me. However, I don't wear the dress for teaching, because Ghanaian women at O'Reilly teach in western clothes.

"Some of the Peace Corps fellows wear *foogoos*, the handsome rough-woven smocks from the Northern Territories. These are attractive and rather like western sportswear. I don't know any, though, who wear the southern Ghanaian clothes. Unless you feel adept with a toga, it might be hard to keep it draped around you. Arnold and I feel intuitively that Ghanaians might feel a white man in such clothes was affected or peculiar.

"We recommend bringing with you a full two years' supply of cosmetics, toothpaste, shampoo and similar personal articles. The department stores and Lebanese stores carry lipsticks—mostly midnight shades—powder, perfumes, but it is extremely unlikely that you will find the brands you like. You can waste a lot of time looking and not finding. We are now mourning our last tube of toothpaste. We still give a casual glance for our brand in new stores, but are becoming resigned to substitutes until we get home. Don't count on having refills sent to you because import duty on cosmetics is a full 100 per cent."

If one is looking for a short summary of what is expected of a Peace Corps volunteer, one would be hard-pressed to find a more descriptive précis than this one, from a girl in the Philippines, again writing home to the volunteers who are about to join the overseas ranks:

"In my opinion, among the main prerequisites for a successful Peace Corps volunteer are: a love of people, courage to try anything once, and a sense of humor. A Peace Corps member in the Philippines must be able to eat any kind of food, i.e., *dinuguan,* made of the blood and guts of chicken; he must 'love' rock and roll music; be an expert at the twist. He must be able to give a speech when he unexpectedly finds his name on a graduation program, or sing a solo, when the only thing he can sing on key is *Jingle Bells.* Depending on his college major, he must be able to give a learned oration to an audience, which may be composed of college students, professors, and even presidents on A Brief History of American Literature, Ancient French Music, Einstein's Theory of Relativity, or the Painting of Picasso. He should be an expert at organizing libraries, curing snake bites, setting up summer camps, teaching swimming, starting home industries, and improving methods of rice production. If by some chance he can't do, or doesn't know how to do, these things, it doesn't matter, he will do them anyway. Besides these extracurricular skills he is most certainly an expert teacher, although he has just graduated from college and taught only one class in his life before entering his own *barrio* school. He of course understands completely all the principles and methods of teaching English the second language way, as well as being a 'whiz' in demonstrating elementary science, though his last science course was high school biology. These last two things are of course his main assignments. Our fond volunteer must happily pin ribbons at athletic meets, coach volley ball teams, and contestants for English declamation contests, and judge music or literary contests, only to find that the prizes in English are awarded on the basis of the most dramatic gestures rather than the understandability of the spoken English. If *he* is a *she*, then she must listen to a great number of beautiful and not so beautiful serenades and dance at the public dances with the mayor and other local residents. Both sexes must be careful to play center field and stay on everyone's good side. As likely or as not, if there are two leading families in town, they belong to two different political parties, and if the volunteer seems to prefer one family, he will be accused of political favoritism. He accepts all invitations to *fiestas* (Feast Days in honor of the patron saint of the town) with joy and eats something at every home (though he is invited to as many as twelve). Seriously, though, it's really wonderful to have had this privilege of living and working and sharing in the life of another country. The natural beauties of the country were a constant inspiration to me—the mountains, ocean, palm trees, rice fields, all so different from anything that I, at least, have ever known."

CHAPTER IX

LOOKING BACK

*A*s *the spring of 1963 approached, the first volunteers were nearing the end of their two-year tour of duty with the Peace Corps. It prompted a number of them to reflect on their experiences overseas, and to make some judgments about what it had meant to the countries in which they were stationed, what their successes and failures had been, and how the experience had affected them.*

One such letter takes a long view of the Peace Corps work in Chile:

"That this work is all success and not discouraging is not true. In fact, it is difficult to see immediate gains. Only now as we look back can we begin to evaluate group and individual progress and, therefore, evaluate our own progress to the extent which we helped bring this about. The fact that I have been trying unsuccessfully to teach the troop guides to put a basic plan of an activity on paper a week in advance and then carry it out is demonstrative of our often slow progress, particularly slow when you evaluate it in terms of North American group work activity. These three guides and their sub-guides are only now, after eight months' work with them, beginning to accept this need for planning and have recently shown some (not much) ability in carrying out their plans alone. You can imagine (or perhaps you can't imagine) the number of times we come home discouraged, frustrated, or simply depressed and wondering if this effort is all worthwhile. Our work has its ups and downs morale-wise, and we get tired, then refreshed; discouraged, then thrilled with signs of progress. Our vacation in the South gave us a diversion and rest, and was a wonderful trip.

"We have access to a cross-sample of newspaper articles from the U.S. about the Peace Corps. We are often concerned about the 'mud-hut' image of the volunteer which the people at home seem to have, and likewise we sometimes get concerned at the hopes the U.S. public seems to put on the Peace Corps as a solution to foreign problems. At its best, the Peace Corps is, in this stage, still only an experiment. At present it is not the answer to underdeveloped economies nor will it make even a noticeable dent. We hope you people realize this.

"Our hope of the Peace Corps includes the basic three-point purposes of the Corps, but more broadly we see other possible outcomes. Maybe something can be learned from this experiment to throw light on the present foreign aid program, something that will make foreign aid a more lasting thing economically for the host country. We hope also that our efforts will focus some attention of the foreign host country on their own problems and motivate them to do more for their own people. There are few, far too few, private charitable organizations in Chile. Some people are embarrassed that we come here to help their people. I wish more were embarrassed. Another thought—to what extent can the Foreign Service utilize returning Peace Corps volunteers? The successful volunteer goes home with much knowledge of the country's problems and procedures at a grass-roots level and is fluent in the language."

Another volunteer, a teacher, evaluates with candor, but also with understanding, the African people with whom he has lived for the past two years. He is left with few illusions about what can be accomplished overnight by the American volunteer, no matter how willing and patient he may be:

"I think that if I were to tell a new group of volunteers anything, I should tell them to prepare for 'the long pull.' I should also emphasize that French is the language in French West Africa, and the better you can get along in it, the better and the sooner you can begin to make headway with your job. As you know, the five of us trained for the Project were reasonably proficient from the start. I majored in French in college, and though I had not spoken it for some twenty years when I joined the Peace Corps, I had always managed to keep using it from time to time; I had not lost all of it. But I realized after I got to my job here at the *Cours Complementaire d'Agboville* how much I should have liked to have had the language better at my command. There was no difficulty in conducting a class. And when I made mistakes in spelling (which God knows I do in English, let alone another tongue!), I was only too glad to have the students correct me. Let me add that the youngsters were only too glad to do it because a teacher that admits to being wrong is a very strange animal. French teaching and pedagogy is something I shall cover later in this letter, however. I was speaking of 'the long pull.' By that I mean that the job our Peace Corps men and women are going to be doing is a two-year, up-hill fight. And I mean the word 'fight.'

"The fight is primarily against what we will feel is African indifference, and French jealousy. I do not think—after much reflection (which I hope is mature) that the African is indifferent—or at least as indifferent as he may appear to be to most of us Occidentals. In speaking of the African character, I think many things must be taken into account. Not the least of these is the incredible monotony of the climate. Twelve hours of day merge into twelve hours of night, and the very birds and beasts move with their own inner clocks! The cocks crow (or begin to crow) at 4:00 *du matin,* and the songbirds start at six sharp in the winter, and ten minutes earlier now that the sun has moved back on our side of the equator. The temperature during the year may vary as much as twenty degrees, but I have yet to see it. And I have had dreams, glorious dreams, of Minnesota winters or Vermont lakes in the early mornings. The monotony of life here is difficult to understand or believe if you have never been exposed to it. There is only the endless joyless sun (as Conrad put it) and the rooms full of fractious kids, so used to the 'cash-register' system of French education that they are going to fight it for all they're worth! It is quite a heartbreaking thing from time to time. But for a person as old as myself it can be quite exciting, too. There are so many things you can do with the youngsters, for—as I say—they've never seen such odd fish as us Americans.

"My French colleagues, and even other members of the Peace Corps, complain of the attitude of these youngsters: they have no idea of work, they expect everything to be given to them. It is true. But I don't think that should influence our attitudes too much. There is a reason for it. These people have a built-in social security in their family life, and they can always go out and pick their food off trees in the forest. A long time ago, I wrote to my father that if the Africans never invented the wheel it was because they never had to get anywhere. They were already there. Through thousands of years they have been in equilibrium with nature. One could live rather like the *cigale* through a brief, glorious summer, and pass on to the lands beyond death. The 'reason' for sustained effort was simply lacking. I spoke to a class recently about life in the U.S., saying that everyone had a chance at education and that after you had completed it, you went to work. There was a silence, and one student raised his hand (naturally, one of the more lovable, utterly lazy fellows). 'What,' he asked, 'if you do not want to work?' And do you know, the question stopped me! I am so used to the Puritan idea that everyone works that, even though I know there are plenty who do not work *chez nous,* the question rarely becomes real to me.

"There is no tradition of such effort here; there never has

been. If a youngster is motivated it is largely because he hopes to have a better suit of clothes or a nicer automobile. The shiny American culture has an enormous appeal on this basis, but it is far from the Greek ideal of restraint and excellence in which I was educated (and which I should like to impart). The Socratic ideal that the unexamined life is not worth living simply falls on deaf ears here. I suppose there are thoughtful students, but I can honestly say that so far I have met none. Here again, however, there is a certain language barrier, for they cannot talk to me in their own tongues, and I cannot talk to them in mine. These judgments must always be taken for what they are worth.

"There is an astonishing lack of humility. This, I feel is cultural. They receive a certain kind of very warm love as children. Life checks them, but their elders seldom do. Perhaps this is at the root of it. But the childish vainglory that you see is sometimes discouraging. They seem like children who are waiting for Christmas plums to drop into their hands. How do you tell them what I learned so many years ago, and which I am so glad to have learned—that nobody ever told me I was to have a particularly good time here on earth, and, never having expected it, I have had a simply glorious time. These youngsters seem always to be looking at the other side of the coin.

"The poverty one sees here is almost inconceivable to an American. Students who go to the *Cours Complementaires* come from all over the Ivory Coast, for it is the idea of the government to mix them up and get the members of one tribe thoroughly used to the members of another. Well and good. I went to visit one of my students not long ago.

He is here from Sassandra, a fishing village about 400 kilometers away. He lives in a mud hut where he shares a pallet to sleep on, a table, a single chair, and a lamp *à petrol* which had no petrol when I was there. There is a single little petrol stove, too, on which he cooks his rice. Food prices for anything better here are exorbitant. The diet is not calculated to make consecrated students. And if you take a walk after the sun has gone down, you'll find under the street lights of the town, those youngsters who do (oddly enough) have some interest in their schooling, learning—memorizing by ear their dear little lessons.

Another teacher explains the importance of being good at one's job—that the Peace Corps volunteer's first duty in this instance was to be a good teacher:

"What I am experiencing right now is interesting because it will happen to any volunteers teaching in *lycées;* the letdown at the end of the school year which fizzles out rather than ending. All year I have worked under pressure to finish the program, pressure to get grades in and cumulatives made out, and pressure in the class to get the students to understand, but at the end of May, with another month of school to go, the school year stops dead for the bac exams. The students who are not taking this exam stop coming to school, and so the teacher is left with an empty classroom and all the work he had planned to do in the month of June. This is only one indication of the general problem: the school career is based on the passing of exams, and any genuine motivation, other than the fear of the exams, is difficult to stimulate. Often the students will complain that anything outside the text is a dangerous waste of time because it will not appear on the exam.

"Because our training had to include so much in so short a time, I came out of it with the idea that a Peace Corps volunteer was a well-informed and roving anthropologist, social worker, community developer, and sometime teacher. The time we spent on the beaches and on trips while waiting to be placed did nothing to change this impression, until one day I walked into a classroom, and for the first time I didn't have a seat with all the other kids. So it meant becoming an all-the-time teacher, and, but for that special problem—language—the classroom could have been in the U.S. For a long time I was 'the American physics teacher' and was sniffed and prodded accordingly. But luckily I found I enjoyed teaching (I had a hunch I would but never knew for sure) and that there were few things more satisfying than to see students suddenly understanding; I think honestly that this has made all the difference for me and for all the volunteers. Without satisfaction in your work it is almost impossible to maintain an interest and appreciation for what you see outside the class, for all that Africa outside the school grounds. The beauty of Africans and the fascination that comes in trying to understand the complexities of their culture and their hopes and fears as human beings is always sustaining if our own frustration and disappointment is not too great. You are right, nothing helps as much as knowing what you are in for and honestly trying to know how you will react to it; one thing is sure though, people who knew or had a good idea that they did not like teaching are not happy in this project because the teaching is that important."

From Sierra Leone, a Peace Corpsman writes of having to search his own values and preconceived notions about education when faced with students who were "industrious and eager to learn," yet "didn't have the background to do what was expected of them."

Despite the frustrations, he believes more than ever in extending "the hand and the heart:"

"For what should a Volunteer be prepared? He should be prepared for a delightful, warm, friendly, appreciative, and fun-loving people, and for the nerve-racking frustrations that arise out of incomprehension and consistent failure. He should be prepared for a rewarding experience which will live with him as long as he is on this earth.

"I know that I have come upon a situation which has caused me to stop and completely reevaluate myself, my ideas about education, and my ideas about a person's integral relationship with his culture. I have always held (somewhat idealistically and academically, to be sure) that there is a certain 'oneness' about humanity which no amount of epidermal coloring or cultural uniqueness could hide. The last five months in West Africa have done nothing to alter that view, except to strengthen it.

"As the Peace Corps idea becomes more real and functional I begin more and more to realize what a rare and wonderful opportunity this whole thing becomes for everyone involved. The need for education in Sierra Leone is desperate, and the appreciation we have been getting from people on all levels is no less than astounding. Some are a little hesitant to believe that we would give up the luxuries of America—the good jobs, the money, and the conven-

129

iences—for that which West Africa has to offer, but they are nonetheless glad to have us. One student (at the College) said to me, 'I really don't understand why you would want to do this, but welcome.' This is not to say that many do not grasp the underlying idealism involved, but many find it difficult to believe that it springs from American soil. I think that the best explanation we can give is an operational one—visible and tangible evidence of Americans living and working here for someone else's interest. The question 'Why did you join the Peace Corps?' that has plagued us all from the beginning becomes increasingly less and less academic. One no longer has to resort to abstract philosophical arguments and platitudes (true as they might be), for I now find myself in the midst of the answer, surrounded by a situation which cries out in self-explanation. The poverty, the illiteracy, the substandard educational opportunities which are rampant in this as well as many other countries are reasons enough for anyone to want to extend his hand and heart in order that these blights might be at least partially effaced."

Finally, this report from one of the project directors, who, by virtue of his position, was able to get a total view of the entire Peace Corps effort in one country—in this case, Chile:

"Though I certainly do not want to imply that our project is going to remake Chile in our 21 months here, I do know that we will leave a mark in many parts of the central valley. Our volunteers have made literally thousands of friends who now know and appreciate Americans as they never had a chance to do before. The dedication, sacrifice, and daily example (especially of the willingness to get out and do manual work, something still far from popular among the educated classes in Latin America) do not go unnoticed by the Chilean. We can hope that the effect of this will be like the dropping of a pebble in a pond.

"Naturally, the conclusion is inescapable that some volunteers seem to achieve a little more than others. Some of this is due to inherent differences in temperaments, personalities, and capabilities. In other cases the difference might well lie in the varying traits of the counterparts. Sometimes the local circumstances are responsible. To combat this latter situation, we have seen fit to make changes in the place of assignment of some volunteers, almost invariably with favorable results.

"Our first year in Chile, then, is over, and in fact this group of volunteers is heading into the homestretch of their two years of service (July 20 being the termination date). As I have tried to indicate, it has not always been easy. In truth, the problems, the frustrations, the crises of one sort or another never cease. This we really knew in advance would be the case. But it does irk us to read occasional newspaper items from the States, penned no doubt by smug individuals sitting in well-heated offices, commenting caustically on what a soft touch the Peace Corps volunteers have, namely, a two-year all-expenses-paid tour to distant spots with $75 a month salted away for them back in Washington. This lack of appreciation of the difficulties inherent in Peace Corps service is both appalling and discouraging. It would be a pleasure to lump

131

all such critics into one bunch and place them in any of several duty stations in southern Chile for the coming 20 months. The resultant cries of anguish and change of tune would be music to our ears.

"For my part, I am proud of all our volunteers for the manner in which they have borne up in the face of all difficulties and all frustrations. As we have known all along, we have a really wonderful bunch of people in our group, and they are showing to better advantage as time moves on. A great change is visible after a year in Chile. As would be expected, our volunteers are now more settled in their work, more adjusted to Chilean ways—and to the possibilities and manner of changing some of them, more experienced and self-assured in what they are trying to do, more adjusted to their counterparts—really more a part of the 'family' is what it amounts to, more familiar with the offices and persons (both American and Chilean) who can give them needed assistance and advice, better able to plan their work. And, of course, some of this works two ways. There is a more relaxed feeling all around as friendship and understanding replace the tentative and questioning attitudes and associations of our first months here.

"It would, indeed, be patently unfair not to express our gratitude for the warm welcome, true appreciation, and constant support that we have received from all the personnel of the IER (*Instituto para Educación Rural*), practically without exception. I have insisted all along that it was a rather sublime act of faith in us for the IER to ask for 45 volunteers at a time when the Peace Corps had barely started and when no one could really say for certain how successful it would be. They wanted us sight unseen and they received us most warmly, though they had to be aware that if the whole operation proved a big failure we could almost literally have ruined the IER. And they have accepted a rather amazing percentage of what we have asked for or recommended.

"As I have stated repeatedly in these pages, our volunteers have had many difficulties and bad moments here in Chile. But they have also had a million laughs, and all of us have stored away enough memories to last a lifetime. And they realize too that their Peace Corps stint is not all a matter of sacrifice and of giving. They themselves are getting a great deal out of the experience. They are certain to return home with true fluency in Spanish, a deep understanding of the customs and problems of a civilization considerably different from their own, and proven self-assurance, maturity, and qualities of leadership. How else could they have developed so much in so short a time? A good number of the volunteers also will return home with something more—a husband or a wife. As of this writing, there are seven engagements in our group. More engagements would seem to be in the offing. So, for these people, it's the Peace Corps and romance as well. Who could ask for more than the opportunity to help some of the world's underprivileged people and at the same time find a life partner?"

CHAPTER X

Thank You for Your Son.....

*N*o more fitting letter could be found to close this anthology than the following, not from a volunteer but from a young Chilean, Raul Gonzalez, of Pucon, to the parents of a Peace Corps volunteer.

"Dear Mr. and Mrs. J. G.

"I apoligize for my poor English but I woul try to do my best in the typewriting.

"I was intended to write this letter to you long ago, as soon as your Jerry came to live with us. to express you how my wife, my little girl, myself and everybody in town and the School like him and all of us are very fond of him.

"His cooperation and charmy personality has beeen a very strong help in our proyect so much that would be very difficult to find other volunteer to be able to take his place after his trip home next July.

"We sorry no to have the confort the foods and the comodities that you have back in the States. Sometime Jerry must walk, ride a horse and expended time wanting for a lift. I think in this way his has the opportunity to learn more about us about our people, our feelings. He is remarcable in getting into the people and they call him in a very warm manner, Mr. Cherry. You know here Cherry is a very popular licuor.

"With my wife we are proud to have Jerry with us and we sey to you that you have a very nice son, how in this very moment is celebrating his 25th birthday. We are trying to represented you, if that can be possible, given him our most kindeness wishes of happy birthday, showing him that for us he is other son from our own. The marbelous work in which Jerry is connected has the previlige to GIVE to the human being who are in contact with, something from our own soul, from our own heart, so you can't forgive as long as you live that all of the poeple, no matter where they came, are friendly people, willing to be hellpful of each other. Specially true is this when the person in charge to this job is like Jerry a very real Embassador, the type of Embassador that we badly need in this present time when the history in no writting in speach, reports and papers articuls but in the battleground itself where we need to fight against poverty, ignorance and misundestanding.

"We are very glad to have Jerry with us and we are happy to say to you that we are very fond of him.

"For him, for you and for the meaning of his effort we invite you to sing for him a very warm 'Happy Birthday dear Jerry'."